Histo[illegible]any of Basingstoke

Essays by

George W. Willis

Collected and edited by

Barbara McKenzie

The Crosby Press Basingstoke 1972

First published November 1972

ISBN 0 903580 00 4

Printed and bound in Great Britain for
The Crosby Press, 26 London Street, Basingstoke, Hampshire
by Chapel River Press, Andover, Hampshire

Since publication it has come to light that a substantial portion of this book was in fact the work of members of the Workers' Educational Association local history group at Basingstoke and not of the late George W. Willis as was thought. Typewritten drafts of the material were among Mr. Willis's papers at the time of his death and the editor of the collection therefore included this material in good faith believing it to be written by Mr. Willis.

TO DOROTHY SCOTT AND EDITH WILLIS
with gratitude

Contents

Illustrations

Acknowledgements

The Editor wishes to acknowledge thanks to the following:

Mrs. Dorothy Scott and Miss Edith Willis (sisters of George Willis) for permission to use their brother's essays.

Mrs. Frances Corfe (née Griffiths) grand-daughter of Mr. J. R. Ellaway, for permission to use the essays written jointly by George Willis and her grandfather.

Basingstoke Gazette, *formerly the* Hants & Berks Gazette, *for allowing me to reproduce articles and notes first printed in their newspaper.*

Wallis & Steevens, Ltd, engineers, for allowing me access to the records of the Basingstoke Canal Navigation Company.

Photographic Acknowledgements

With one exception, all photographs contained in this book are from the collection of Mr. R. L. Brown, to whom grateful thanks is here recorded.

Editor's Foreword

When George Willis died in February 1970, at the age of 92, Basingstoke lost not only a Freeman, magistrate, historian and archaeologist, but also a philanthropist and friend. Certainly no one knew Basingstoke as well as Mr. Willis did, and possibly no one cared about the town quite as much as this loved and respected man.

I was honoured to be given many of his personal belongings and notes by his two surviving sisters, Mrs. Scott and Miss Willis, in order that I could write his biography; amongst his possessions were a lot of notes pertaining to the history of the town. Some of these had been given as talks to the Rotary Club, the local Churches and organisations during the last 50 years; some had been printed as articles in the local newspaper, which had been jointly written by George Willis and his friend Mr. J. R. Ellaway; one or two had been written with Mr. H. Rainbow. Some of these historical essays, as far as I can ascertain, have never been read publicly. Obviously years of research went into the compiling of them, and it is clear from his personal notes that George Willis had intended to complete a history of the town he so dearly loved. It is typical of him that in 92½ years he did not have the time to do all he wanted to!

Thus it is with the greatest pleasure that I have collected and edited these notes into this *Historical Miscellany of Basingstoke*. I must emphasise that I have altered Mr. Willis' own words as little as possible, and added even less.

The Willis Museum is, of course, George Willis' greatest gift to his town, but I hope these collected essays will supplement the exhibits in the Willis Museum.

Hook, 1972 S. Barbara McKenzie.

Preface

"I remember old Basingstoke" by G. W. Willis

(Reprinted by kind permission of the *Hants & Berks Gazette. Editor's note:* although not published until later, from his personal notes and records this appears to have been written by George Willis in 1952, when he was 74.)

Over the last sixty to seventy years Basingstoke and its district has grown and changed, and has trebled its population and altered from a quiet agricultural centre to its present industrial pattern.

Seventy years ago Basingstoke was a more or less compact town and was surrounded with real country of estates and farms—and farms were farms—with cowman and dairymaid gradually replaced through the years by chauffeur and parlourmaid. Compared with the countryside of 1890 the trimmed hedges and artificial road surfaces make it today like a park.

The town then seemed to have assumed a static and permanent form compared with the rapid changes of the past thirty to forty years. The Market Place was a quiet stone cobbled area only disturbed by the iron tyred wheels of passing carts. At one period these cobbles were replaced by wooden sets on a concrete base, but I recall that technical difficulties seem to have arisen, as in wet weather this wooden flooring rose in large shallow bubbles due to the expansion of the wood blocks.

Besides the weekly markets, as held today, the market place was crowded with stands and stalls once a year at Michaelmas Fair on October 11th and 12th. There were peep shows, little roundabouts and especially a boxing booth where unwary countrymen were invited to try their luck against the brawny boxer who displayed his muscular development on the outer platform. The Fair was an event of some importance in an agricultural community as the hiring of local farm labour ran from Michaelmas to Michaelmas. Farm workers, seeking re-employment lined the main street wearing their distinctive emblems, a tuft of wool for a shepherd, or a twist of whipcord for a ploughman. After Michaelmas, farm carts could be met carrying the family and furniture of the labourer to the farm of his new employer.

Occasional occupants of the Market Square were batteries of artillery on their way to their annual practice at Okehampton. Men and horses were billeted at the local inns while the guns stood under guard in the Square overnight. Their departure in the morning attracted considerable interest among the younger generation, but their passage along the so-called water-bound flint roads of that day was disastrous. I remember trying to cycle to Overton soon after the battery's departure, to find the road two inches deep in flint dust from hedge to hedge, the hedges also covered with thick white dust.

Before the advent of tar and its successors roads were formed of loose flints broken to about $1\frac{1}{2}$ inch diameter, spread over the roadway, and before the later advent of the steamroller, left to get worked in by the traffic, such as it was. With adequate rainfall and traffic this method often resulted in a fairly good road surface, but not in a long dry spell. In the town the dust was laid by the municipal water cart, a large horse-drawn tank with a long spray attachment behind it that periodically paraded the streets, often turning the dust into mud.

Street lighting was by gas, and by modern standards could only have been "better than nothing". The square glass sided lanterns held an ordinary fishtail gas jet of very limited illuminating power. These had to be lit and extinguished by hand and the lamplighter was a familiar figure, quickly trotting from lamp post to lamp post with his pole over his shoulder, which carried at the top a metal case sheltering some form of naked flame. The advent of the incandescent mantle immensely increased the efficiency of the lighting, to be followed by the convenience and intensity of electric light.

The water supply of the town came from the town well in the Steam Dell in Reading Road. I can recall being shown by the engineer, Mr Drummond, the beam pumping engine in the engine house there—both engine and house have long disappeared. This was probably the last beam engine in the district.

That the town escaped serious epidemic can be regarded as a miracle, as a contemporary report on water supply described a very foul well, bricked off from the town well, with many leaks in the brickwork! The new well at West Ham was then being sunk and the clank of the contractors' pumps during the fortnight of the final test of the well's output could be heard all over the town. As a youth I saw through the doorway of the new pumping station the starting of the new engines by the then Mayor. When, after the First World War, the station was doubled in size, I was the Chairman of the Water Supply Committee.

The installation of the town sewage system with its incredible disturbance and inconvenience to town life, the deep trenching of the streets and burrowing under houses was fortunately before my time. I do recall the laying of the subsoil drain along the bottom of the town to take off the excess of water in the valley gravel beds. This drain has never failed to deliver millions of gallons of water per day into the River Loddon beyond Vinces Farm in the Basing Road. It had one unfortunate effect in that a water main was fractured in the process, the town water became contaminated and a serious typhoid epidemic followed which taxed the accommodation of the Infectious Diseases Hospital, and gave the town an unenviable notoriety.

The town has expanded very unevenly. To the east on the London Road the last houses were the White Hart and Eastlands, the latter standing in its own grounds that extended to Dark Lane. Where Eastrop Lane now runs was a deep sunken lane, overshadowed by high trees, down which women were excusably frightened to go after dark. This lane passed over the canal by a humped bridge and continued up Gas House Road. It is difficult to understand where traffic could have come from that could cut so deep a roadway from the London to the Basing Road. A similarly deeply cut lane existed earlier alongside the present London Road from the top of Dark Lane. This was probably the original road out of the town and was superseded by the present artificially cut London Road. Note the causeway across the marshes beyond the Common, the deep cutting up Wellock's Hill and the wide curves between the King's Head at the Hatch and Nately Scures Hill, so dangerous to modern traffic.

Up to recent years an iron railing bordered the footpath from the White Hart to the large Common gate, to protect pedestrians from the cattle passing to and fro daily from local dairies to the Common pasture.

The Canal, at one time a pleasant amenity of the town, has now disappeared as far as Basingstoke is concerned. I well remember hiring a boat at the end of the black path from Goat Lane to Eastrop Lane and rowing up towards Basing. Not far beyond the bridge was a well known bathing place. In the winters of long ago it was often possible to skate at Basing and beyond, as well as on the Black Dam, Hackwood Park Basin and Popley Fields Dell.

One of my happiest schoolboy memories is that of walking down the London Road to the Hatch, getting on to the Canal bank and walking home along the towpath. The seemingly endless summer day, the sunshine on the quiet water, the shoals of fish, the flowers and the blackberries remain one of the warm recollections of my youth.

Another pleasant schooltime memory is the discovery of Bedlam Bottom, a secluded valley beyond Farleigh Hill. Incited by a paragraph in the *Hants and Berks Gazette,* a schoolfriend and I, before our cycling days, walked through Cliddesden up the footpath past Farleigh Church, across the Park down into Bedlam Bottom. This quiet and remote meandering valley, shrouded in woods, drowsing in the August sunshine left a lasting impression on me, and made an early contribution to my appreciation and enjoyment of natural beauty which has given me so vivid and permanent a pleasure in later life.

The Railway Station of my youth was approached from a much smaller station yard than the present one by a flight of steps up to an outside platform from which one gained the inner platform via the booking office. I, in common with other travellers, was once mysteriously ushered off the platform into the booking office and the door was locked. On looking out at a waiting train I saw the reason for our dismissal. At the window of a compartment sat a grey haired old lady; Queen Victoria was waiting for her train to be shunted on to the Reading line.

The widening of the main line from Waterloo to Southampton meant a substantial reconstruction of the station to its present shape, and was not without its difficulties. The embankment between Hook and Basing persisted in slipping outwards until checked by extensive pile driving, while the cutting between Hook and Winchfield persisted in slipping inwards until effectively drained by intercepting channels. Little of the original station remains; the iron roofed part of the subway and some of the building on the northern platform may belong to an even earlier station than the one I knew.

Down Sarum Hill the last building on the left was the British School, now the Baptist Church. Beyond it lay fields lined with acacia trees right away to Downslands House, and beyond, fields again. On the right side, houses stopped at Rayleigh Road, with the Grammar School, Beech Lodge, Highfield House and West Ham House this side of Worting. Beyond Rayleigh Road my way to school led between high banks covered with bushes and shrubs and crowned with high trees that I recall were very picturesque under snow. In the field between Rayleigh Road and the school cattle grazed. I once saw an Italian showman walking along Rayleigh Road leading a very tame and shabby dancing bear. The cows saw them too, for suddenly they all raced to the roadside fence gazing fearfully at the bear, with their tails all extended horizontally. I have never been able to understand what primitive instinct can have evoked such curious conduct, as it is unlikely that they had ever seen a bear before.

I recall the construction of Penrith Road for a special reason. The field sloping down to the stream was cut into a depth of six to eight feet and the excavated soil thrown out to form the level roadway. Examining this distributed soil I found it contained abundant burnt flint, which I traced to a six inch black layer forty feet in diameter at the bottom of the excavation, which could also be seen in the sides of the sewer trench in the middle of the road. This was undoubtedly the site of a primitive cooking site, overlaid by thousands of years of rainwash from the adjoining slope.

The British School, with its Junior Department below, now the Domestic Science School, was promoted by non-adherents to the Anglican Church and its income, apart from donations, was derived from weekly school money brought by the children who were assessed on their parent's occupation at sums varying from two-pence to four-pence per week. This school, with the National School in Cross Street, was closed when the Board Schools were built in Fairfields. Before this building, open fields extended down to Southern Road, where the rough edge of the meadow bordered the pavement.

I remember seeing a flock of sheep in this meadow, probably the last remains of the sheep fair held on the old fairground, which had been granted to the town in the Enclosure Award in 1786 in lieu of its right of holding a fair on the open downland at Kempshott.

I was present at the official opening of the new Board School, as a member of a class deputed to sing a song at an appropriate period in the programme. As this involved sitting quietly during all the other items of a long afternoon, which to us consisted of a dull unintelligible mumbling from the main hall, I can still feel the boredom I suffered during that day's proceedings.

I was also present at a later date when the first sod was cut in the construction of the Alton Light Railway. This was officially performed by the President of the Board of Trade in the presence of the Chairman of the South Western Railway and others. The President's concluding words seem to have impressed me: "I hope that the energy and enterprise of the South Western Railway will meet with the success that energy and enterprise always deserve". From the eventual fate of this unfortunate line it would appear that energy and enterprise do not always get their deserts.

Considerable building was taking place in my early days in the Solbys Road area. The developer, Mr. Tyrrell had lived in Essex, and the roads in this area carry the names of Essex villages, Solby being the name of his former residence in that county.

I can well remember the first motor car that came to Basingstoke; it was a Coventry two-seater owned by Mr. F. Watson of Wote Street. It had features strange to the modern motorist, open flame ignition and a gearbox in which the lowest gear was represented by a pinion 1½ inches in diameter, working into a gear wheel about twelve inches in diameter—a gear which Mr. Watson proudly told me would take him up any hill in the district. The silencer, if any, must have been less effective, for seated one day at the top of Nately Scures Hill, I clearly heard the approach of the Watson car as it passed the Kings Head at the Hatch.

I was kindly invited by my namesake, Mr. Willis, to hear what was probably the first wireless set in Basingstoke. Its capacity for crackling and distortion was enormous. Any personal movement near it disturbed it, and it had to be nursed at a distance by means of long vulcanite rods, but the voices from London did come through. I remained very thrilled to realise that I had heard someone speaking in London without any apparent connection between us.

The first rubber tyre, other than cycle, I recall, was a solid one fitting into an iron rim on the wheel of a dog-cart; it seemed at the time, the very essence of luxurious travel.

The first cinema film in the town was, I believe, an advertisement film of Sunlight Soap, shown free of charge at the then Corn Exchange, now the Haymarket Theatre. When the show opened we saw a rather dingy, yellowish still of vehicles and pedestrians on a London bridge. Then suddenly they all started to move, and I well recall the "Oh" that went up from the crowded audience. The picture flickered terribly and the film was old and scratched, but to unsophisticated Basingstoke it was wonderful.

The first time the marvels of X-rays were demonstrated in Basingstoke was at a lecture in the Town Hall, possibly one of the Gilchrist lectures of fifty years ago. To be able to see a key shut in a handbag, and even the bones of one's hand seemed the realisation of the impossible.

I must share with many others the recollection of Brinkletts Car Park as a deserted farm yard with derelict buildings and implements. But not so many will remember the old Manor House opposite, behind the present Manor House and surrounded by trees. This earlier house was occupied by Mr. J. Mares, who subsequently demolished it to make way for his new Manor House. This proved to have been built too close to the main road, but at that time the railways had appropriated both passenger and goods traffic, and Winchester Road was hardly more than a country road used largely by farm carts and tradesmen's vans.

I should like to think that others of my contemporaries may be induced by these random recollections to add their own contribution to the record of the town as they knew it in the days of their youth.

I George W. Willis (1878–1970). This was taken when he was 90 years old

II Bronze spearhead, 7 inches long and weighing $5\frac{1}{4}$ oz. found close to the Roman Tile Kiln at Hook in gravel. This was identified by the British Museum as late Bronze Age, circa 650 B.C.

III The Roman Tile Kiln at Scotland Farm, near Hook. This was excavated at Easter 1970 and destroyed a few weeks later by contractors digging gravel for the construction of the M3 Motorway (Photograph by Barbara McKenzie)

1

Basingstoke in Prehistory

Little enough now remains to remind us of our heritage from the times before the written histories. A visitor to the Willis Museum, Basingstoke will see displayed there some of the artifacts of man, made and discarded or lost by him, over a period of at least 100,000 years.

Where then, may we look for such traces of past cultures, other than in the museum, and how are the sites of archaeological finds related to the type of countryside surrounding our town?

What is now the Rural District of Basingstoke embraces two distinct types of terrain. To the north lie the clay soils, heavily wooded in ancient times, damp and unyielding to the hand of primitive man. To the south are the chalk lands covered then by light woodland and scrub. Here and there however, are the patches of clay-with-flints, capping the higher ground, which gave rise to dense forest. These areas, now cleared to the plough, provide some of the best arable land in the chalk-rich areas.

On the chalk downlands was to be found a ready supply of flint from which to fashion crude tools and weapons, so that in Palaeolithic times (100,000–12,000 BC) flint working sites were set up here, and most of the recorded finds come from the southern half of our district. Many worked flints have been found; many more must remain yet to be discovered. A diligent search across a newly ploughed field will often reward the eye, without perhaps, offending the farmer.

In 1912, Penrith Road was constructed near and parallel to the line of one of the branches of the River Loddon, at the bottom of Sarum Hill. Here were open fields sloping gently to the banks of the stream, which may still be seen from Bramblys footpath which joins Penrith Road to Bramblys Close. Near to the stream were found unmistakeable signs of an ancient cooking site, with a blackened flint hearth. This discovery came to light after a number of finely worked flint flakes were noticed on a nearby spoil heap from the road working. This must be the first evidence of a man-made settlement, albeit of a temporary nature, in Basingstoke itself, and was in use at least 5,000 years ago, in the Mesolithic period (12,000–3,000 BC).

During this period, a milder wetter climate prevailed and the different hunting conditions occasioned by the southerly migration of the great animals led to the production of these smaller, finer-worked tools. Although man was still essentially nomadic, some habitation sites were set up now near to the source of food at riversides, or ponds and adjacent heathland.

The last of the Stone Age people were the Neolithic invaders from the

Continent (3,000–1,800 BC) and they introduced the first serious attempts at settled farming. Camps were constructed on the chalk uplands surrounded by a causeway dug into the chalk; the scrub and light woodland were cleared and areas of pasture and corn cultivation established. A primitive community was in being, and the foundations of village life were laid.

These people buried their dead together in chambered tombs dug and fashioned from the chalk rock and its thin mantle of soil. One such "long barrow" has been preserved within the Borough boundaries. In Kempshott district, in the angle between Pitman Close and Seymour Road is a low grassy mound, forty-six yards long, twenty-seven yards wide and nearly a yard high. A plaque at the edge of the mound proclaims that this site has received the somewhat belated distinction of a Preservation Order by the Ministry of Works and Ancient Monuments. Much degraded by the effects of time, and with its surrounding ditches obscured by the new roads and houses, here is a link with the people living perhaps four thousand years ago.

In the Bronze Age (1,800–550 BC) a different people had different ideas on the right and proper way to bury and honour their dead. The practice of single burials under a circular earthen mound, known to us as a "round barrow" patterned the landscape of our gentle hills. In fact, these barrows form the most numerous of the prehistoric field monuments which survive to this day; in Hampshire alone there are nearly one thousand! Several examples are visible within our area. Some have been excavated; this was a favourite pastime in Victorian days when many barrows were desecrated, and their contents lost forever, in the search for gold ornaments which occasionally accompanied the interments. Other barrows, more properly examined, have yielded articles such as beads, bronze rnaments and pottery. The local museum has several such finds on dısplay and prominent amongst the exhibits are the burial urns in which were held the cremated ashes. Many of the barrows have been ploughed down or otherwise degraded. The present occupiers of 191 Kempshott Lane may like to know that a barrow was levelled to make way for the house that now stands there!

A burial urnfield was discovered at Middle Down near Dummer which contained many individual urn burials spread over an area of downland, but without the accompanying earth mounds. Also of local interest were the graves dug into the chalk found when the railway cutting for the Great Western Line from Reading was being prepared in the last century. These were situated near to the site of the Reading Road bridge, and two reports of the discoveries appear in the *Hants and Berks Gazette* in 1882 and 1883.

During the Bronze Age, the footprints of man began to leave a permanent mark on the chalk uplands as trade routes developed, which linked the southern counties from west to east, and from north to south to the prehistoric ports. Most of these ports were to be found between Portland Bill and Selsey Bill. It has been said that it is the tragedy of British prehistory and history, and the key thereto, that the most habitable and most easily conquerable areas are adjacent to the shores whence invaders are most likely to come. Back and forward along these routes passed the merchants and pedlars (Chapmansford, near Hurstbourne—the ford of the pedlars) keeping where possible to the higher better drained ground and shunning the heavy clay to the north.

Two trackways passed through our area from the west, possibly converging near to Basingstoke and continuing eventually as far as the coast of Kent. The first of these is a familiar name to those people living in the southern outskirts of Basingstoke—the Harrow Way. The origin of the name is not certain. The Anglo Saxon chronicle for 900 AD mentions the Hoare or ancient way. *Herewag* is a Saxon name for a military road, and yet another possible derivation is from the word *hearweg,* meaning "road to the shrine". Certainly the route passes close by the great monument of Stonehenge.

The Harrow Way enters Hampshire from the east near to the remains of a Norman castle called Barley Pound, following the line of the modern road to Well. About half a mile south-east of Well, it forks into two branches that converge again twelve miles west of Oakley. The longer southerly route was probably taken in the winter time for it is a route following higher ground. The more direct northern way later superseded the original parent ridgeway, and has now become known as the Harrow Way. This coincides with the road going north-west from Well to Long Sutton and Four Lanes End, on the Odiham to Alton Road; then on to Five Lanes End and Polecat Corner. The ancient way now forms the minor road along the north edge of Hackwood Park, crossing the A339 and joining the A30 as far as the Stag and Hounds Inn.

Here the A30 turns south-west but the Harrow Way is represented by Pack Lane (a significant name) and after crossing the Roman Road to Silchester north of Kempshott village, the line is traced by minor roads to meet the B3400 and on to Oakley Station. Somewhere here it was joined by the southern branch to complete the loop. The combined route then follows the by-road going to Kingsdown Wood and turning south-west to cross the modern way to Kingsclere, takes the line of the lane which cuts the A34 one mile north of Whitchurch.

It may be of interest to note here that a minor road just west of Oakley Station leads north-west from the Harrow Way, and we may trace the line of a trackway skirting Great Deane Wood to Freemantle Farm, south of the village of North Oakley and on to meet the North Hampshire Ridgeway at White Hill.

Returning to the southern branch of the Harrow Way, this is shown by the lanes running to Sutton Common (one and a half miles south-east of South Warnborough) and then by a metalled road to the Golden Pot on the A32. Turning north-west, the branch continues as a footpath through Western Common and on Nash's Green. Here it bends south-west through Bagmore and thence north-west by road and path to Ellisfield. The next village is Farleigh Wallop; then the track crosses the B3046 and heads by road and path again to tumulii (round barrows) near the A30. We lose the route now for some distance until the lane to Pardown and the road to Oakley past the church. Hereabouts the loop is closed, as mentioned, to the northern branch.

The other trackway to pass into this area is the North Hampshire or

Ink Pen Ridgeway. From the Seven Barrows which are one and a half miles south of Burghclere, close to the A34 Newbury to Whitchurch road, the track climbs to Ladle Hill and follows the ridge past Sydmonton Park and Watership Down to White Hill. Then the route runs to Cottington's Hill and south to Hannington; the course is now the road which runs just south of Ibworth, then as a lane three quarters of a mile south of Upper Wootton to Whitedown Cottages. Finally the track meets the minor road to Sherborne St. John and the line is taken up by the A339 to Basingstoke —the latter once being known as Dyers Down Lane. It is not certain whether the track merged with the northern branch of the Harrow Way, or whether it continued independently from Basingstoke, but it is more likely to have joined to follow the natural land passage through the Test/Loddon divide at Basingstoke, leading into Surrey.

The gradual introduction of iron into this country from the continent heralded the extension of settled farming on the downlands, and the threat of further invasions gave rise to the great defensive earthworks, the hill forts. A cluster of Iron Age (550–150 BC) settlements grew up around the Winklebury hillfort and to the east and north, on the slopes down to the clays beyond. Their distribution at this time shows that the modern road branching from the Harrow Way at Oakley, and passing through Worting and Basingstoke to Hatch, was also a trackway. To the south-east of Basingstoke are woodland sites at Bradley and Budd's Hill, near Preston Candover. A chalk downland site occurs at Bulls' Bushes, south of Oakley; east of the town evidence of habitation comes from Wellocks Hill.

The people who came to establish these farms brought with them the Celtic language, ancestral to the Welsh tongue. They developed further the trackways which now connected the chains of hill-forts. For example, the North Hampshire Ridgeway included the forts of Walbury, Beacon Hill, Ladle Hill and Winklebury. So, for this period, sites of both a pastoral and military nature are recorded. The pottery, and the contents of rubbish pits once used for grain storage, give us an insight into the mode of life of these people. The area of the Rural District is rich in such signs of habitation and one may expect more to come to light with the excavations prior to building the estates for the new Basingstoke.

Three hill-forts are to be found within our area; at Sherfield, Winklebury and Ellisfield. The fort at Sherfield, known as Bullsdown Fort, can hardly be described in the same context as the other two as regards its siting. The north edge of the camp follows a contour only 200 feet above sea level, with a stream, the Bow Brook, a few hundred yards to the south. The soil here is clay and the drainage poor. The site occupied an area of ten acres and had a double bank and ditch defence, which was oval in plan. The entrance was on the north-east side, but is now destroyed; the fort is covered today by a dense wood.

The camp at Winklebury stands on the 400 feet contour line with a commanding view to the south over the Loddon valley. It was one of the earliest forts in the country, pottery sherds dating from the third or fourth century BC being found in the rampart ditch. There was a single wall and ditch enclosing about nineteen acres with an entrance somewhere on the east. The oval shaped fort is very much mutilated, and soon no vestige will remain, for a new school complex now occupies the site which was once the stronghold of Iron Age Man.

Near to this camp is the Lunway which enters our district at Totford and makes its way along green lanes and minor roads via Bradley to Herriard Common where it joins the south loop of the Harrow Way. The actual junction could have been a little west of Bagmore, providing a good reason for the siting of Ellisfield camp.

The last immigrants to arrive before the Roman occupation were the Belgic tribes, who had been ousted from Gaul by the Romans and who were in consequence forced to seek new settlement areas. The Atrebates from the Artois district of Belgium, reached Wessex from the Selsey area and established their tribal capital at the place now known as Silchester. So that, at Calleva Atrebatum (the city in the wood of the Atrebates) for the first time, the higher chalk land was forsaken for the lower wooded ground. Traces of the ramparts of pre-Roman Silchester with a ditch and counterscarp and enclosing about ninety acres have been seen on aerial photographs. Excavations have exposed a flat bottomed ditch with sloping sides forty-five feet wide at the top and twelve feet wide at the bottom. At the bottom of the eleven feet deep ditch have been found pre-Roman pot sherds, and Belgic hut foundations which have been exposed on the south side of the earthwork. In addition to this, moulds for coins and Arretine pottery ware have also been uncovered.

The Belgic invasion which reached Wessex about 55 BC does not seem to have displaced the previous population. This is evidenced by finds of pottery from early Iron Age to Romano–British on the same settlements, for example at Worting Road, Chineham, Daneshill, White Lane and Cholsey Farm. There are, of course, some new Belgic settlements, such as those at Monk Sherborne, West Farm (Popham), and in the woods of New Farm, South Warnborough. A settlement has recently come to light on the Oakridge 2 estate, where much pottery and some animal bones have been recovered from ancient ditches and rubbish pits. A well, cut down into the chalk for a depth of more than seventy feet, has yielded a wealth of material, including pottery of a distinctive type known as New Forest Ware, in association with both animal and human skeletal remains. The site was obviously in occupation at, or about the time of the Roman Conquest.

2

The Roman Era

Before Caesar carried out his two reconnoitres in 55 and 54 BC, Commius, who had already come up against Rome on the other side of the Channel, led his tribe, the Atrebates to Britain. They had landed, probably near Selsey Bill and had made their way northwards. Nearly a century later, at the time of the Claudian invasion of AD 43, they were the most powerful tribe in the area south of the lower reaches of the Thames, probably of all southern Britain, their rivals in power being the Catuvellauni, centred on the area which is now known as Hertfordshire. The tribal capital of the Atrebates was at Calleva (now Silchester) some eight miles to the north of the modern Basingstoke.

The Romans made a practice of using the local tribes, not only as a means of local government, but also as a means of Romanisation. Just as Winchester was known as Venta Belgarum (Venta of the Belgae) and Caerleon as Isca Silurum (Isca of the Silures) so the tribal capital of the Atrebates became known as Calleva Atrebatum, the wooded town, Calleva of the Atrebates.

Detailed consideration of this place must lie outside the scope of this essay; suffice it to say here that it was the seventh largest town of Roman Britain, the tribal capital and the centre of local government for a large area (how large is not certain) and like most Roman towns it was an important centre of communication. From it main roads went via Staines to London, to Winchester, Salisbury and Cirencester. One of these, the Silchester to Winchester road, passed close to where Basingstoke now stands, a part of its course to this day is called the Roman Road, running from Worting to near Park Prewett.

The three and a half centuries from AD 43 were a period in which the Basingstoke area, like most of the country, enjoyed a higher level of civilisation than it had ever known, or indeed was to know for some considerable time afterwards. No longer did fresh waves of invasions necessitate hurried defensive works, as at Ladle Hill; no longer did inter-tribal warfare mean that the local inhabitants needed to be perpetually on their guard against ambitious or hostile neighbours. Although the northern and western parts of the province of Britannia were military zones, with garrisons at York, Chester, Caerleon and on Hadrian's Wall, the southern part of the country knew a peace it had not known before; the "Pax Romana" meant that trade and agriculture could flourish, and Britannia became one of the granaries of the Empire. The majority of the population undoubtedly lived lives which, in their essentials, were little different from their earlier ways; town life was for a small privileged minority, and only the leaders of Celtic society could afford to adopt Roman ways, living in town houses, or villas in the countryside. These villas varied greatly in size and importance. Some, such as the great villa at Chedworth in Gloucestershire, were centres not only of farming but of industry; some, such as that at Rockbourne, near Fordingbridge in Hampshire were obviously country dwellings of some importance, both as centres of great farming estates and as the residences of wealthy Romano-British or Roman officials. Many, however, were of much less importance, and many of the places marked on maps as "Roman villa" would be better marked as Roman buildings for not all were residences of importance, indeed some were little more than farms with perhaps one or two of the attributes of a villa, in most cases maybe only a hypocaust (central heating).

The area around Basingstoke was the subject of a study in Romano-British population development by S. Applebaum, published in the proceedings of the Hampshire Field Club and Archaeological Society in 1951. He describes the area as a "reasonably representative stretch of southern English countryside", with thirty-eight known sites with Roman structural remains such as roof tiles and wall plaster, of which twenty-two have some evidence of hypocausts, Wheatsheaf and Stanchester being of primary importance. Settlements in several places (such as Daneshill, Buckskin and Steventon Manor) seem to have ceased during the first century AD, this probably being connected with the appearance of a Roman house at Newtown, west of Basingstoke. At other places, however, sites inhabited by the Britons before the Roman Conquest continued to be occupied, such as South Ham Farm and Park Prewett (probably a cemetery), although these may well have been of the estate based on the Newtown villa. A Roman building of some sort existed near the Wheatsheaf Inn, south of Basingstoke; it has been suggested on rather flimsy evidence that this may have been a temple, but it is more likely that it was merely a farm (or inn?) which owed its importance to its position, that is, half way between Winchester and Silchester, in fact at the crossing of the Winchester to Silchester road and an earlier trackway. Several other villas (the term is used in its widest sense to mean any country house or farm) were founded shortly after the Roman Conquest, and there must have been some increased farming activity; North Warnborough and Balchester being the most noteworthy locally. There was a quieter period of steady growth before a more prosperous period in the third and fourth centuries, with occupation being renewed in several places previously abandoned, Old Basing, Andwell and Worting Road among them. This, Mr. Applebaum suggests was probably because the Newtown villa extended its area of influence, many satellite holdings springing up around the estate boundaries.

Since the heavier soils to the north remained largely uncleared of their forests until the time of the Saxons, the chalk downlands to the south of Basingstoke were the most important agricultural lands. Since streams and springs are comparatively few, the area would have been unable to support large numbers of cattle without considerable work in well-digging. The size of the Roman well at Basing House, however is a warning against underestimating the ability of early farmers. On the whole though, we are probably justified in thinking that grain-growing and sheep-rearing were the chief occupations of the farm inhabitants. It is when we come to decide just how many inhabitants the area supported that the difficulty arises, partly because of the difficulty of deciding the size and nature of the "villas", and also because historians have long argued over whether to allow 50, 100 or even 200 inhabitants for a large villa, or whether 50 should be allowed as an average figure for population of a villa and 12 for all lesser places showing signs of occupation. Using several different methods for the area south of Basingstoke, Mr. Applebaum arrived at the conclusion that the population was between 9 and 12 per square mile in the later Roman era.

Nearer the Loddon, where there was no shortage of water and where the swine could use the forests for foodstuffs, the population may well have been twice this estimated figure, particularly as these inhabitants would have had easier access to Silchester, a ready market. It must be remembered that "Basingstoke" did not exist; the area was an agricultural one within the sphere of influence of Silchester, the tribal capital, the centre of government and taxation, and the great market town of the area.

One question remains: what happened when the Anglo-Saxons came? No detailed evidence has been found to enable us to be sure when Romanised life in this area ceased but late fourth century pottery at Stanchester, and a late fourth century coin at the Wheatsheaf villa suggest that to the south anyway, the old life continued until then and there are some grounds for thinking that it may have continued elsewhere. It is probable, however, that as the fourth century progressed, the area declined into what has been called a "sub-Roman twilight", with people in one or two places trying to maintain the old standards in an increasingly insecure world. The place-name Woodgarston (near Monk Sherborne)—"Wealagaerstone"—in 945 suggests a possible British survival, but on the whole we may accept that with the decline of the Roman civilisation, Britain entered the "Dark Ages", a period difficult to describe because of lack of evidence, but without doubt it was a period when civilisation was on a much lower level.

Editor's note: I have deliberately not altered the author's notes, but during the construction of the M3 Motorway in 1968 and 1969 further excavations were possible at the Wheatsheaf site. Numerous pottery sherds, coins and other finds gave much more information than was previously known. Amongst other things, in a small workman's hut there was a heap of over 100 sandal nails, so the settlement was large enough to have its own sandal-maker. I was also involved in excavations at Common Plantation, similarly now *under* the Motorway. At Scotland Farm, near Hook, a Roman tile kiln of the fourth century was excavated at Easter, 1970, only to be destroyed by twentieth century machinery a few weeks later in order to extract gravel for the Motorway construction.

3

Medieval Basingstoke

For an understanding of the evolution of the government of our town, we must go back to Anglo-Saxon times. Wessex, one of the kingdoms of Anglo-Saxon England, eventually established itself as the most important of these, and Winchester became the capital of the country. One of the constituent shires of Wessex was Hamtunscire, the name by which it was known from AD 757. Like other shires, Hamtunscire was split into smaller divisions called hundreds, which were units of a hundred families. These were further subdivided into tithings, which consisted of ten householders.

The responsibility for looking after the king's interests and maintaining his authority throughout the county rested with the shire reeve (sheriff); the word "reeve" is derived from an Anglo-Saxon word "gerefa" meaning a steward. The sheriff conveyed to the towns and hundreds the writs and precepts which came from the king and saw to it that they were carried out. He was also responsible for the maintenance of law and order; this he did through the agency of the County Court, over which he presided, and the hundred courts, which he visited as necessary. His influence and authority extended down into the tithings, where he saw to the holding of "views of frank pledge".

The king's interests included those of a landowner. In the period immediately preceding the Conquest, the king was in fact the chief landowner in Hampshire, owning not only the city of Winchester but also estates scattered throughout the county, for example at Andover, Hurstbourne and Basingstoke. Another important landowner was Earl Godwin, the Earl of Wessex. Estates were also held by the Church and one of the leading owners was the Bishop of Winchester.

Landowners kept to themselves such parts as were necessary for their own use, renting the rest to tenants, in return for an annual payment either in money or in kind or both, the lands retained by the owner were called "terrae dominicales", from which we derive the term "demesne lands". In addition to the free tenants, who paid money rent and helped the owner at the busy times of the year, there were unfree tenants (villeins) who performed a weekly labour service for him.

For these estates the Normans introduced the term "manor", which is derived from the old French "manoir". This originally meant a dwelling or residence but from the time of the Domesday survey onwards it came to be used for the lands held by a lord or important personage.

Domesday describes Basingstoke as "always having been a royal manor". The king is said to have the town in demesne, that is to say, he kept it in his own hands, not letting it out to tenants. The manor is described as consisting of 20 villeins, 8 bordars, 12 ploughs, 6 serfs and 12 freemen. It also had 3 mills and a market. The annual revenue from the mills was the same as from the market, namely thirty shillings.

The manor of Basingstoke was not itself part of a hundred; instead it had as appendages (appurtenances) the hundred of Basingstoke and five other hundreds, those of Bermondspit, Chuteley, Holdshot, Odington and Overton.

The functions of the sheriff of which we have the clearest record are those concerned with the collection of revenue. This consisted of rent from the different manors and also of sums collected in the form of fines levied at the various courts, as well as taxes such as aids and tallages. Details of these are recorded in the documents called the Pipe Rolls. Some of the story of Basingstoke in medieval times can be reconstructed from extracts taken from these.

The town is first mentioned in a roll in 1159–60 (6 Henry II), when it is recorded that the sheriff at that time, Richard Fitz Turstin, had paid into the royal treasury the sum of 66s. 8d., which represented fines for murder in the Basingstoke hundred.

In 1168, Basingstoke contributed £8 13s. 4d. towards an aid levied to raise money for the marriage of the King's daughter, Matilda. An aid was a means of raising money to meet particularly heavy demands on the king's exchequer; it was customarily levied on the freemen of the manor. Other rolls of the same period show that fines were paid for various misdemeanours: for example, in 1175, John the provost of Basingstoke was fined 20s., "because he had denied what he afterwards acknowledged". It would be interesting to know the details of this, but it is not recorded. What is important is that this appears to be the first reference to the office of provost, from which we may assume that the town enjoyed at this date a measure of self-government.

In 1186–87, a tallage, a tax similar to an aid, was levied on all the king's demesnes. Basingstoke was assessed at £14 9s. 4d. The town paid only half that sum, the remainder being paid in two instalments in 1190 and 1191. This seems to be the beginning of a period of indebtedness for the town.

The year 1195 saw John de Basinges owing a fine of 20s.—for selling wine contrary to the assize. This meant that what he supplied was not correct in amount or of satisfactory quality. It may also have meant that he was charging an unfair price. It is to be regretted that there was a repetition of the offence, for in 1197 it is recorded that he owed 13s. 4d. for another infringement of the assize.

In 1203, the fifth year of the reign of King John, there is an entry which refers to the market of Basingstoke: "The town of Basingstoke owes two marks, which they had offered so that the market which was held on a Sunday should henceforth be held on Monday". Two years later we find the town owing £6 16s. 0d. for amencements, which were fines, the amount of which was determined arbitrarily by a court not prescribed by statute. No detail is given of the offence which caused them to be levied, but it is recorded that only £4 was paid in settlement. It also appears from the roll of this year that William, provost of Basingstoke, owed 10 marks for a purpresture, by which we are to understand that he had enclosed or encroached on the property of someone else; he was permitted to settle this amount in instalments.

The year 1211–12 was an important one for the men of Basingstoke, for in this year the king granted them the "firm of the manor". This meant that they were themselves directly responsible to the king for the payment of the rent of the manor, without reference to the sheriff. From the roll of that year it appears that they paid a rent of £104 12s. 0d. for the term of the manor of Basingstoke with the six adjoining hundreds. However this arrangement did not last, for the men of Basingstoke found difficulty in paying this sum regularly, and so in 1217 the custody of the manor was granted first to Bartholomew Peché and then later in the same year to Luke de Drumare. By 1221 the situation had again altered, for in that year the roll records that the men of Basingstoke rendered an account of £104 12s. 0d. for the rent of their town with the six hundreds. "The above rent seems to have been burdensome to the town, and the accounts become complicated in consequence". In 1225 the sum of £186 2s. 1d. was still owing. One result of this continuing indebtedness was the separation (in 1227) of the town and the hundred of Basingstoke (the inner hundred) from the five external hundreds, which the king retained in his own hands. This allowed the men of Basingstoke to hold the manor at a reduced rent of £80. However the financial problems of the town were by no means solved by this arrangement, for it is recorded that in 1230 the sum of £209 9s. 4d. was outstanding. The town was ordered to repay this by annual payments of £20 beginning in 1231, "but they still managed to get into arrear". Recourse was had to borrowing as is shown by an entry in the roll of 1236. There it is recorded that three of the men of Basingstoke were summoned to explain to the king's justices why they had borrowed the sum of £20 in the name of Basingstoke and without their consent.

In 1237 Walter de Burgh was appointed the king's bailiff, with the responsibility of looking after the finances of the manor of Basingstoke. He seems to have been no more successful than others in obtaining payment of the annual rent.

The roll of 1238 mentions for the first time the name of Walter de Mertone in these words:

> "Walter de Mertone accounts for the 15s. for the term of the lands and tenements within the demesnes and services of the manor of Basingstoke, held by the said Walter, to be paid by himself and his heirs to the Exchequer annually at Michaelmas".

In 1240 Walter was granted the manor for five years at an annual rent of £80. At the end of this period it again became the responsibility of the sheriff. This remained so until 1256, the year in which Henry III granted to the men of Basingstoke and their heirs the perpetual tenure of the manor and hundred of Basingstoke. By this charter the men of Basingstoke became responsible for returning their own writs and summonses independent of the sheriff. In practice this meant that the town was from now on nominally a self-governing community. However more than a hundred years were to elapse before the town received the power to act as a corporate body.

THE ANCIENT JURISDICTION OF THE MANOR OF BASINGSTOKE: HUNDREDS AND PARISHES

OVERTON HUNDRED

Laverstoke
Overton
Deane
North Waltham
Tadley
Bradley

CHUTELEY HUNDRED

Monk Sherborne
Hannington
Church Oakley
Wootton St. Lawrence

BASINGSTOKE HUNDRED

Bramley
Sherborne St. John
Chineham
Eastrop
Basing
Basingstoke
Hatch
Kempshott
Cliddesden
Winslade
Tunworth
Mapledurwell
Up-Nately
Nately Scures
Newnham
Steventon

BERMONDSPIT HUNDRED

Dummer
Farleigh Wallop
Nutley
Preston Candover
Ellisfield
Herriard

ODINGTON HUNDRED

Upton Grey
Weston Corbet
Weston Patrick
Hoddington
South Warnborough

HOLDSHOT HUNDRED

Stratfield Mortimer
Silchester
Stratfield Saye
Stratfield Turgis
Hartley Wespall
Heckfield
Eversley

Notes

The hundreds of Overton, Chuteley, Holdshot, Bermondspit and Odington were those separated from the Manor and Hundred of Basingstoke in 1225.

The Hundred of Odington was united with the Hundred of Bermondspit in the fourteenth century.

N.B. in Domesday, Basing is included as part of Basingstoke Hundred.

4

Walter de Merton (1200–1277)

In Basingstoke between the years 1200–1205, a son was born to William and Christina le Kuk, or, as is now more commonly known, Cook; the baby was the only son among seven daughters. This son they named Walter after his paternal grandfather. Walter's mother Christina Fitzace was an important woman who held lands here; her family were freeholders on Crown Lands within the Royal Manor of Basingstoke.

When he was quite a small lad, Walter was sent to Merton Priory in Surrey to be educated. Later at Mauger Hall, Oxford, Walter was known by the name of his birthplace, Basingstoke, until 1233 when he took the name of the Priory, and as Walter de Merton (sometimes spelt Mertone) became Parson of Cuddington. Between 1231 and 1263, Henry III was showering lavish gifts and vestments on Merton Priory, thus it is not difficult to see how the Prior's Clerk from a Royal manor with a skill in conveyancing and law should have found his way into the Royal Chancery.

Between 1236 and 1240 or 1242, Walter went into the service of Nicholas Farnham, Bishop of Durham, and during these years travelled many miles between London and the north. When Bishop Farnham resigned in 1249 Walter returned to the south to become King's Clerk and Chancellor. Henceforward the Court and the capital were to be the two main bases of his operations.

Walter was made a Canon of St. Paul's in 1259, and from November 1272 until August 1274 he was in place of the King holding the great seal of England, not only as Chancellor in fact, but virtually as regent. A number of letters written to him by Edward I and Queen Eleanor still survive to this day. In July 1274, Walter was elected Bishop of Rochester.

Despite his fame and achievements, Walter never forgot his family and his home town. His first foundation, the Hospital at Basingstoke, commemorated his mother, and the second, Merton College, Oxford, was originally dedicated to the education of his kin. The hospital came in for a share of Walter's charity and munificence. He liberally extended its area and erected more suitable buildings as well as a chapel, then took steps to ensure its permanency, by placing it under the king's protection.

Walter's parents were buried in St. Michael's Church, Basingstoke, quite near to his hospital "which stood on the north side of the town brook, a little below the bridge".

The spring of 1275 found him again at Merton Priory, where he drew up his will. It was a long and careful document. He gave consideration in this to his kin, friends and servants, and remembered too the benefices he had held.

The will can be enlarged upon:

Total bequestal in money	£2,014 17s. 0d.
Articles valued at	£ 711 8s. 6d.
	£2,726 5s. 6d.

The provisions made by a wise and pious man for the College of Merton can be seen by the course of study for the year 1274:

1. Grammar
2. Arts and Philosophy
3. Theology for all after proficiency in Arts
4. Canon Law, for four or five select proficients in theology.

On the eve of the Feast of Ss. Simon and Jude, that is, Wednesday, 27th October, 1277, Walter de Merton, Bishop of Rochester died, and there in the Cathedral of Rochester he is buried, in a twice restored tomb in the north-east transept. He is recorded as having died "after fording the Medway". Merton College, Oxford, the oldest of the remaining Oxford Colleges, is responsible for the repair of the tomb; the present alabaster effigy dates from 1598.

He was six feet tall, so physically the founder of the Basingstoke Hospital and Merton College, Oxford, was a giant among his contemporaries.

The man is long since dead and forgotten, but the name in Merton Road, Basingstoke lives on.

5

Fairs and Farming

Fairs had played an important part in the life of the town and in the life of the surrounding farming community ever since 1449, when Henry VI (in a charter) gave the town the first grant of a fair. It was to be an annual fair held near the Holy Ghost Chapel, lasting from Wednesday to Friday in Whit Week. The Charter of 1622 mentions two fairs, the Whitsun fair and another on the feast of St. Michael. This Charter also confirmed the holding of a market on Wednesday of each week. Those attending the market were to be able "to buy and sell all kinds of merchandise, and all beasts, goods and chattels at their will according to the laws and customs of England". The 1641 Charter repeated this in slightly different terms: "all coming to the market may be able to buy and sell all and singular goods and merchandise, grain and wool and all singular beasts, goods and chattels at their will according to the laws and customs of our realm of England, paying reasonable tolls and customs to the Mayor, Aldermen and Burgesses . . .".

The earlier grant of two fairs was increased to four in 1671, when Charles II granted two new fairs to be held on Basingstoke Down. The first of these was held on the Tuesday and Wednesday after Easter, the second on the 10th and 11th September.

By the early nineteenth century, however, there were at least two fairs, but it is not clear just how many. In 1841, for example, there was an Easter fair, at which there was "a fair supply of cattle, including milch cows at high prices", pigs were abundant, as also were horses, but these were not much in demand. To judge from a report in the *Hampshire Chronicle* of September 1840 the September Fair seems to have declined over the years: "The sheep and cattle fair, formally held on Basingstoke Down previous to their enclosure, and since that period held in a very limited field set aside for that purpose, took place by permission of the Trustees, on the Common last Wednesday, and was well attended by dealers and breeders, the supply of sheep being very considerable, which went off readily at prices similar to those at Wilton. The revival of this fair, in the midst of so extensive an agricultural district as that which surrounds Basingstoke appeared to give universal satisfaction to the numerous breeders and dealers attending it, who expressed the determination to support the same by every means in their power . . ." despite another important fair, namely Wherwell being held the following day.

It was also held on the Common in the following year. The weather on this occasion was not good, 5,000 head of stock were penned and 4,000 were sold. The brief report of it added that there was also a ready sale of carthorses.

IV Basingtsoke Railway Station, about 1900, before the Great Western Station was united with the London and Southampton Station. Picture shows the Great Western Station, which later became premises for the Railway Social Club now moved to modern premises

V The Railway Arms in Brook Street

VI   The Holy Ghost ruins, from the interior

VII   17th century houses in Chapel Street

The farming of the district was under the benevolent encouragement of the North Hampshire Agricultural Society, the fore-runner of the Royal Counties Agricultural Society which celebrated its centenary in 1961. The North Hampshire Agricultural Society was active in encouraging good farming by putting up prizes for competition. A notice of the annual general meeting of the society, which appeared on 12th April, 1841, mentioned that a good sum of money would be distributed as prizes "to shepherds, shearers and other meritorious labourers". This was quoted as an indication that those who were better off were "not regardless of the comforts and necessities of the honest and industrious peasantry".

The society also made awards to farm servants for other reasons. For example, sums of up to £5 were given to married men who had brought up a large family with the least assistance from parochial relief. Awards were also made to female servants and to single men under 30 for length of service with one master.

The Basingstoke weekly markets had always been in addition to the annual fairs. Right from the earliest records in Domesday, there is mention of a market being held on Sundays. In 1203, the day was changed to Monday and in 1214 Wednesday became market day, "in order that this market may not be injurious to other markets". It appears to have been a Wednesday market day for Basingstoke since then. In the nineteenth century the weekly markets for grain and stock were well attended by farmers and dealers from a wide area. The 1837 report says that they came from Andover, Winchester, Reading and Newbury.

A special Act of Parliament in 1829 resulted in the Basingstoke Cattle Market close to the (then) new railway; and the cattle market on this spot remained for nearly 140 years. During the life of the cattle market, the main market continued at the top of the town but as one of the first parts of the new Basingstoke, a second market square was built at the lower end of the town within months of the closure of the cattle market.

6

The Open Fields and their Enclosure

Pre-industrial England had primarily an agricultural and peasant society. The mass of Englishmen down to the nineteenth century earned their bread by cultivating the fields which lay around their villages and towns. When we speak of towns in this pre-industrial age we really mean overgrown villages, whose tradesmen and craftsmen gained their livelihood in part at least, by cultivating these fields and by grazing their livestock on the town common.

Basingstoke was no exception. According to the census returns of 1801, only fifteen years after the enclosure award was made, it consisted of only some five hundred inhabitants. From the map of 1762 of the town of Basingstoke we can see how each house had its own garden while around the town and along the banks of the Loddon lay the crofts and closes. Beyond, the open fields stretched as far as the parish boundaries.

It would be these great open fields that would give the modern traveller his greatest surprise if he were able to see the Basingstoke of two hundred years ago, used as he is to the patchwork quilt effect of the modern English landscape.

Opposite Deep Lane at the top of which in 1762 stood a barn, began Salisbury Field, and this field stretched as far as the parish boundary with Worting. Above the small hedged crofts and closes along the North Brook, Chapel Field extended to the parish boundary with Sherborne St. John; its only landmarks, amid the farmers' innumerable strips were the Holy Ghost School and ruins and the Winklebury barrows. A short walk up the Reading Turnpike road would have taken us into the North Field. In the south of the parish lay Hackwoodfield and Hatch Field, while to the west Winchesterfield straddled the old Salisbury road. In the south-western corner towards Kempshott were the open grazing lands of the Downs.

The open fields dominated the landscape. Although not entirely treeless and hedgeless, an observer would gain the impression of wide open spaces, while the compact area of human settlement would have seemed much more isolated than today. The lanes and bridle paths which were no more than beaten earth tracks in parts surfaced with chalk, wending their way through them into the neighbouring villages, would seem irrelevant details. The Down overgrown with gorse bushes and stunted trees and shrubs must have given a wild aspect to the scene. It is easy to imagine why an observer like Defoe, travelling through Hampshire in 1724 described the countryside as a "black desert".

At the time of the Enclosure Act of 1784 there were six fields, but we can reasonably assume that originally there were three fields according to the normal pattern corresponding to the three course rotation of winter crop, spring corn and fallow, as practised in open field husbandry. Later as was quite usual, these three original fields became subdivided with multiples of three, and as stated, by the eighteenth century, Basingstoke had six.

In the William de Birteworth terrier which was drawn up about 1300 (certainly after 1240) four fields are mentioned: Northfield, Southfield, Middlefield and Westfield but this record is confusing. It is not at all clear whether Southfield was a sub-division of Middlefield or a separate field, in fact it could be that this was the time when the original three fields were first being subdivided. To make matters even more confusing, in the Merton College Charters which are earlier than the William de Birteworth terrier, there is mention of an Eastfield!

However in later terriers, land was listed indiscriminately under field and furlong headings.

FIELD AND FURLONG HEADINGS IN THE TERRIERS 1300–1578

c. 1300	c. 1409	1444	1543	1578
Middlefield	Eastfield	Southfield	Hackwoodfield	SE Hackwood
Northfield	Middledon	Kyngesfurlong	Hatchefield	SW Hatch
Westfield	Southfield	Westfield	Winchester Field	SW Winchester
Southfield	Westfield	Northfield	Wofield (or Salisbury Field)	W Salisbury
Millfurlong	Northfield	Medefurlong	Holy Ghost Field (or Northfield)	N Holy Ghost
	Nordon	Northdene	Nordon	NE Nordon
	Mullefield			

Assuming that there were at one time three fields we can make a tentative reconstruction of their position and extent by referring to the map of the Enclosure Award and examining the local topography. Basingstoke nestled in the Loddon Valley in the extreme east of the parish. The river runs in a west/east direction, so the slope from west to east is gradual, whereas the land to the north and south of the river slopes quite steeply. Well before 1300, all this land, except of course the grazing and meadow land, must have been brought under the plough. We do know that William de Birteworth in the 1300 terrier owned strips of land on the south side of the Herepath (Harrow Way) and towards Prevet (Park Prewett). We can thus postulate an original Northfield extending over the area later covered by the Chapel and Northfield of the Enclosure Map of 106 and 116 acres respectively. These would lie on the slopes to the north of the Northbrook, and bounded on the north by the parishes of Sherborne St. John, Sherfield and Eastrop. The original Westfield would be shown as Winchesterfield of 560 acres, and Salisbury Field of 406 acres in the Enclosure Map, bounded on the north by the Loddon and the west by the

Roman Road. On the higher ground in the south of the parish extending towards Basing, Farleigh Wallop and Cliddesden was situated the original South or Middlefield, which was shown on the 1785 map as Hatchfield of 451 acres plus Hackwoodfield of 422 acres. This would give us three fields roughly 800–1000 acres altogether.

We do not know for certain when the subdivisions of the three original fields were made. Their division in any case would not effect the crop rotation, and it is improbable that, in the early days at least, their boundaries were permanently fixed. Poor harvests would have meant that additional land taken in from the fallow or waste would have been put down to spring and winter corn. The Winchester College terrier of 1543 shows that the division of the arable into these six fields had already been established.

From the terriers we can reconstruct a picture of how an individual's holdings were scattered throughout the open fields. Their positions in the fields were indicated as are the names of the freeholders or tenants holding strips adjacent to or abutting those of the landowner in question.

This system of holding land in strips scattered throughout the field was introduced by the early English settlers, although it may pre-date the Roman occupation. The Iron Age/Belgic Celts who began their immigration about 75 BC knew the heavy wheeled plough which the Anglo-Saxons brought with them, and aerial photographs have brought to light fields ploughed in long narrow strips of this early date.

The Anglo-Saxons however, introduced this agricultural system whereever they settled, so that it became universal, although in the west it was superimposed upon a Celtic culture of isolated farms and hamlets. Here, as in Kent, the holdings became consolidated and enclosed at a very early date. Basingstoke however, belonged to the nucleated village, and later enclosed country of the east.

The Saxon plough with its team of sometimes eight oxen was forced to plough around an opening furrow as the implement only turned a furrow to one side. To avoid waste of effort, it became imperative that the furrow-length should be great, and the headland, around which the plough turned, kept as short as possible. The strip was simply a day's work, and might consist of more than one land according to the lie of the land. The usual size was twenty roods long by one rood wide, that is, one-eighth acre.

Strips were distributed to each part owner of the plough team in turn but later came to be considered as belonging to one particular person and could be sold, leased or rented. The fields were kept open, for to have individually hedged each man's strip would have been wasteful of man-power, land and resources and would in any case, have made common grazing impossible.

The furlongs, or blocks of strips, which ran in one direction, were all named. These names and the positions of the strips were as well-known to the inhabitants of Basingstoke as the names of streets are in the modern Basingstoke. They were not, however, marked on the Enclosure Map or mentioned in the Award, and have for the most part been lost. Preserved in the modern form from the 1300 terrier are La Fuleflode and Le Kynges-furlong which were in Westfield, also La Holigoste, La Wiltenishbury and

Northdone in the Northfield. (Le Bury and Kingsfurlong were probably once the ancient demesne lands.)

The growth and evolution of the fields before the thirteenth century remains a complete mystery. The arable at the time of Domesday in 1086 consisted of twenty ploughlands, so that if we take the unit at the usual estimate of 120 acres, only two-thirds of the land surveyed by the Enclosure Commission was then under the plough. The woodland which we were told provided for twenty hogs, was then more extensive. From Domesday also we learn that the three mills were already in existence, which seems to show that the valley bottom had already been cleared and was under cultivation.

We can safely assume that it was the land on the hills to the north and south which was still scrub and woodland, given over to grazing and used as a source of fuel and timber. A possible interpretation of Norden (Northdene) is North hill swine pasture. From this evidence it seems likely that the inhabitants first brought the valley bottom into cultivation and then tackled the hillsides, a pattern which has been followed by the more recent building.

Some clues as to the early settlement can be gleaned from the course taken by the parish boundaries. While the boundary with Eastrop and Sherfield, with its frequent short stretches and right-angled turns suggest that the strip cultivation already existed when the parish boundaries were drawn, the western boundary formed by the Roman road indicates that this was an artificial frontier drawn through uncultivated territory.

Before the three fields came into existence the more primitive two field agriculture was almost certainly practised in Basingstoke. It has been established that half of the Hampshire parishes retained two fields until the thirteenth century. Barton Stacey kept them until 1757, when they were enclosed. We know that a third field was created at Hinton in the thirteenth century.

The two- and three-field systems are different not in kind but only in degree. The cropped field in the two-field system must have been in two parts, one for winter sowing and one for the spring; this contains the germ of the three-field system. There is evidence of a prior two field system in Basingstoke. From the 1300 terrier we learn that Nicholas Martin held 57 acres of arable in Le Middlefield, 26 acres in Le Northfield and 23 acres in Le Westfield. The discrepancy between the size of the holding of the first named and the other two would suggest that the Northfield and Westfield holdings were originally those of a single field.

Besides growing corn to provide bread and beer, and flax for his linen, the self-sufficient Basingstoke farmer had to raise livestock for meat and milk. Cattle were raised for their meat, milk, hides and for the making of butter and cheese. As the Middle Ages progressed, sheep raising became more important, for the wool and not for mutton. Oxen were used as draught animals.

The livestock were grazed on every available open space not under the plough: the woodlands, wastes, meadows, crofts and at certain times even the fields themselves. As more and more land was brought under the plough, the common grazing lands of Basingstoke became restricted to the extreme south-west, towards Kempshott, marked on the Enclosure Map as The Down. The name has been preserved in modern times as in Down Grange Farm. In 1786 it was 631 acres in extent.

Although referred to as wastes, the type of land was what we today would call rough pasture. The land in this part of the parish was obviously the most unsuitable as arable land, the chalk in many places just a few inches below the surface. Here the inhabitants of Basingstoke turned out their sheep and cattle in one large herd for permanent pasture.

The Down also provided the inhabitants with firewood; the common right to loppings and clippings and to collect furze (called firebote, or later estovers) was mentioned in the Enclosure Award. A new road laid down by the Enclosure Commissioners called Fuzzy Drive possibly followed the old pathway which people used to reach the firewood. Heath and furze were in any case encouraged to grow because they provided a poor but never-failing source of fodder to a land always dangerously near to being overstocked.

The first known mention of The Down in a document is from a View of Frankpledge held on 17th November, 1464, when we learn that John Wallop of neighbouring Farleigh Wallop had "entered the common pasturage of the Lord King Edward . . . called the Basingstoke Heath alias Shepedown".

In the eighteenth century horse races were held on The Down, and after 1671 the two annual fairs which were formally held "about and near the Holy Ghost" were, through Charles II's grant held on The Down until the Enclosure Act.

The permanent pasture of The Down was not the only grazing resource. In the three course rotation one third of the arable was kept fallow each year while from the Award we learn that "the proprietors of houses and tenements enjoyed a right of common in the stubble from time of harvest until All Souls' Day". This was the day when winter ploughing began.

. . . . .

Basingstoke and Up Nately were two out of nearly three thousand parishes whose open fields were enclosed during the period from 1761–1844. In the period were passed some 2,500 enclosure acts dealing with four million acres. In North Hampshire the parishes of Dummer, Monk Sherborne, Upton Grey, Basing, Mapledurwell, Preston Candover, Nutley and Sherborne St. John were enclosed during this period.

Basingstoke lay on the edge of the "champion" or classical open field country of the eastern midlands, the country of nucleated villages. It was a region of mixed husbandry where grazing rights were highly prized. We can see that quite a sizeable block of this North Hampshire countryside retained its essentially medieval character down to the last half of the eighteenth century.

Although events at Basingstoke were part of a general agrarian revolution which was to affect all the still open-field areas of England, we do not know from which quarter the initiative for enclosure in Basingstoke came.

Basingstoke was not one of the parishes which fell to the strong movement towards enclosure for sheep farming in the period from 1450–1550;

it was too large a parish. There was no one man who could have bought up or otherwise appropriated the whole of some 3,500 acres.

There are no records either to show that attempts were made to bring about enclosure by private agreement during the period 1550–1750. In fact before the seventeenth century, enclosures of parcels of common land were definitely discouraged. In 1511, an individual was fined for having "hedged in part of an acre from the common field". At the same court it was brought to light that "master vicar hath part of an acre hedged in, that was sometimes Baron's land and of the common field, that first was hedge in by Thomas Andrew, and if this be right, others will close in much more which is as yet common field".

In 1540 a bye-law was made "that none shall enclose about the town upon pain of forty shillings". But the following year it was declared that "Thomas Barnard has enclosed contrary to his own and his neighbours agreement".

In 1557 another was fined "for not removing the fence which he had erected upon a parcel of land and thus enclosed it, whereas it ought to be open and be common, like the common field called the Holy Ghost Field".

Of course there must always have been some more independent individuals who wished to break free from the restrictions of a communal agriculture, like the man who in 1511 "hath sown this year in Millfields, that should lie fallow with Hachwode field, contrary to rights and customs".

In the period from 1607–91 we have records of a small number of licences to enclose being granted. At Laxton there was a strong tendency to enclose around 1630 and local opinion favoured this if it was in no way prejudicial to the common wealth enclosures of arable land and were made on the edge of the open fields. These enclosures can be seen on the 1762 map, sometimes a single strip surrounded by a hedge.

The terriers do indicate an increasing tendency towards consolidation of strips, that is of owners obtaining possession of two or more adjacent strips. In 1300 for example, William de Birteworth owned an estimated 76 strips in the common fields and they are all described as being within the three roods to $3\frac{1}{2}$ acre range. In the 1443 terrier however, appear plots of 5, 6, $7\frac{1}{2}$, 16, 20 (3) and even 30 acres among the prevailing acre and half-acre sizes.

We are unfortunate in not possessing a map of Basingstoke fields in their pre-enclosure state, but a picture of their lay-out can be obtained by a reference to the map of the strip fields of the neighbouring parish of Sherborne St. John printed in the proceedings of the Hampshire Field Club (Vol. XVI, p. 257) in an article written by W. E. Tate. In the Church End field among seventy small strips of mostly a big acre or half an acre, there were two large plots of sixteen and fourteen acres respectively. These both belonged to Charles Chute, who with Brocas owned by far the greatest number of plots, but they were seldom grouped together. In the West field, which was divided into three smaller fields or furlongs, there were some 163 plots, again mostly small strips of half to one acre size and mostly belonging to Chute or Stubbs, but among them were six or seven larger plots of 10 acres belonging to Brocas. This is a similar sort of picture to the one we gain from the latest terriers of land held in the Basingstoke fields.

By 1788 all this had been changed by an Act of Parliament. Before the actual Parliamentary proceedings some general meeting of the principal landowners, of which we have no record, must have been held, possibly in 1784 to draw up the petition for the promotion of the Bill.

Although his name was not mentioned in the Bill, one would hazard a guess that the Bill was promoted by the Duke of Bolton, the biggest land-owner in the parish, but we cannot rule out the possibility that the other chief land-owners and tenants pressed the Duke of Bolton for an enclosure. Some of the names mentioned in the Act, the Earls of Dartmouth, Portsmouth and Northington were those of the biggest land-owners in Hampshire. It was, of course, the great land-owners who stood to gain the most by enclosure. Although we must not assume that all the men mentioned in the preamble were necessarily adepts of the "new farming" they were well aware that a more systematic exploitation of their estates by modern tenant farmers, would mean increased rents. The Duke of Bolton's estate was almost entirely let out to large tenants. The main obstacle to individual enterprise was the communal agriculture of the open fields.

The preamble to the Bill was worded in the orthodox formula that as the common fields, downs, pastures, meadows, waste lands and other commonable places in their present situation were incapable of any great improvement, it would be very advantageous to the several persons interested therein, if the same were divided or enclosed; five commissioners were appointed to set out, divide and allot the common fields.

After a standing Parliamentary order of 1774, notice of the petition had to be given to the whole of the inhabitants of the parish. It was usual for such notices of general interest to be placed on the door of the Parish Church. We know from the award that notices were affixed to the south door of St. Michael's appointing meetings to be held about enclosure questions.

We also know there was considerable opposition to the Bill. Among the Churchwardens' records is a letter dated 29th January, 1786, written by Henry Barton the Warden of Merton College to the Reverend Thomas Sheppard giving evidence of a counter petition the previous year, signed by some eighty freeholders and leaseholders, including Anne Attwood, the Merton College leaseholder, and by the Mayor and seven other members of the Corporation. From the parliamentary proceedings themselves as recorded in the Journals of the House of Commons we learn "that the parties concerned had given their consent to the Bill (except the proprietors of about 654 acres who did not choose to sign the Bill, but made no objection to the enclosure, and also except the proprietors of about 160 acres who had given no decisive answer).

The opposition was of course powerless to prevent the Bill from being passed, for only the consent of the owners of three quarters of the land was required, and these as we shall see were only a small minority of the men concerned. They were the absentee landlords with little direct local interest but with the most to gain from enclosure. In any case the machinery of Government was now in the hands of these men. Gone were

VIII The Almshouses in Chapel Street (1891–1965)

IX The lower end of the original Wote Street in 1904. This is now the site of the New Market Square, and it is of interest to note that at least one of the trees shown in the photograph remains

X Brook House, Brook Street in 1964

XI The Fire Station, Brook Street, which was in use from 1913–66

XII Church Square, before bomb damage of 1940

XIII St. Michael's Church, as seen from the Garden of Remembrance

XIV New Street, showing Wagstaff's shop and John Mares factory, in Edwardian days

XV Church Cottage, at the back of St. Michael's Church

the days when a John Powlett could be amerced for "encroachment at Newermes" as happened in 1483!

After the petition for enclosure had been presented to the House of Commons on 2nd March, 1786, the parliamentary proceedings continued in their pre-ordained course until the Bill received the Royal Assent on 16th June. (By 1st May the Bill had been prepared; the Committee stage was reached on 15th when petitions were usually heard). The Act in its final form contained a special proviso about the situation of the Russells Allotments, and one that the lands in the Hackwood Field were to be allotted to the Duke of Bolton. (The Russells lands later became Goldings Park and is now the Memorial Park). It is possible that the Russells had appeared before the committee to present a petition, the details of which are not now available. The Duke of Bolton obviously wished to extend his Hackwood Park, which adjoined Hackwood Field. We know that there were two amendments to the original Bill.

In the sitting in the Lords only twenty peers were present, but no one seems to have been directly interested in the Bill.

Once the Bill had been passed, the Commissioners began to replan the whole of the countryside surrounding Basingstoke. With the help of the surveyor the whole of the land had to be surveyed, the strips and plots of each individual owner had to be quantified, valued and re-allotted in compact fields; new roads and fences had to be set out; land had to be earmarked as a fairground, provision made for a resthouse and workhouse and chalk pits had to be dug. Attention was given to adequate drainage of the ancient meadowlands of Wildemore; compensation made to the Vicar in lieu of tithes; and to those who owned no land but officially were able to pasture their livestock on the commons and stubble fields, allotments were made to the Mayor and Aldermen as Lords of the Manor.

It was a mammoth task, and as an act of planning as radical as the twentieth century new town plan. As two hundred years later, we older inhabitants of Basingstoke experience a quite natural concern over an equally radical transformation of our town similar consternation must have been experienced by our ancestors in 1786. The petition of the Mayor and other Basingstoke folk must have been due, in no small part, to a natural fear and dislike of change.

Of the Commissioners themselves we have little knowledge except their names: John Poore of Andover, Thomas Hasker of Chineham, John Ewen of Froxfield, Richard Bloxham of West Deane and John Carter of Kingsclere.

In the enclosure award, a Thomas Hasker was allotted one acre, two roods and 27 perches in Wildemore. Later, in 1801 an act was passed forbidding the appointment of interested parties as Commissioners; although the ultimate authority came from Parliament, it does seem that the Commissioners were nominated locally, possibly by the petitioners. It is interesting to note that Henry Barton complains in his letter of the "extensive and unlimited power of the Commissioners", and their arbitrary proceedings "in favour of some of the inhabitants". The letter shows that in parishes where the college held large estates they were unable to nominate a commissioner. The Commissioners' authority was in fact unrestricted but how impartial they were one will probably never know. Their sworn affidavits include the phrase "without favour of affection to any person".

More research is possible into the situations of the various allotments of the awardees; one can assume that the lands were fairly valued and quantified. The award states that "exchanges (of land) were made by and with the consent and approbation of the said Commissioners and be ascertained for the more convenient situation of the owners". A full list of such exchanges is set out in the Award.

The Commissioners must have begun work after June 1786. It was a long job and the award was not finally signed until September 1788. In the meantime one of the Commissioners John Poore and George King the surveyor had died, probably from some epidemic disease and they had been replaced by William King and Robert Stones.

The Award itself is kept in the Borough Archives, while among the documents held by the Trustees of the Common is a copy of the Enclosure Act and an extract from the Award bound together. There is also in existence a map showing all the allotments. The new allotments and the old enclosures are numbered, with the names of their owners written in the key at the side. The map also indicates the positions of the old open fields.

When we come to the allotments in detail we find that there were surprisingly only 55 proprietors whose shares ranged from the thirty-two perches allotted to Mary Cooke, to the Duke of Bolton's which was just under 750 acres, that is between a quarter and a fifth of the 3,519 acres, 3 roods, 8 perches surveyed and planned by the Commissioners. The next biggest proprietor was the Earl of Dartmouth with some 418 acres, followed by the Vicar, the Reverend Thomas Sheppard with 262 odd acres, Pembroke College with 215 acres and Harriet Brocas with 207, so that we can say that the six biggest proprietors owned between them over one half of the parish.

The next class of proprietors, that is those who owned between 100 and 200 acres numbered ten, and included Merton College, Winchester College, Peter Searle, John Limbrey, John Davies and the Holy Ghost Chapel (of these John Limbrey held 316 acres, in addition, from the Duke of Bolton).

Next in order of size of allotments came the Curate of Horsepath fifty-four acres, Earl of Portsmouth seventy-five acres, James Hardy, M.D., sixty-seven acres, and John Covey sixty-six acres. Excluding the allotments for the Common, and lands awarded to the Corporation, a further eight allotees were awarded allotments varying from thirteen and a half to forty acres. The remaining twenty-six proprietors between them were awarded seventy-six acres, so that it can be seen that about one half of the proprietors owned barely 2 per cent of the Parish land.

Examining the names of some of the smaller freeholders enables us to see that they were not necessarily small peasant proprietors. For example John Byford, who was allotted only eight acres (and most likely the son of Giles Lyford, last Mayor of Basingstoke in 1769) was a canal proprietor. Eight of the smaller allotees (acreage ranges from one to seven) were indicated as Baronet, Lord and Esquire, and included such names as Lord Rivers and Sir John Tylney Long. The Mays, Mary Pitman, Mary Olliffe,

John Covey, Frances and William Russell can be classified as belonging to the town oligarchy. These surnames all occur in the lists of Mayors and Aldermen for the seventeenth and eighteenth centuries. William Pink (allotted 2 acres, 15 perches) was described in the 1784 Hampshire Directory as a brandy merchant.

Thus it looks as if the land was already owned by three classes of proprietors, the great absentee landlords, the Colleges and the richer town men. The small peasant proprietors had already been almost if not entirely squeezed out long before the Enclosure Act.

One can perhaps detect in the opposition to enclosure a conflict between the interests of the oligarchy (local men always striving to base their power on landed wealth, families such as the Mays, the Coveys, the Lyfords, the Olliffes, the Pitmans and the Russells) and the colleges (always conservative in agricultural practices) on one hand, and the big absentee landlords (such as the Duke of Bolton and the Earl of Portsmouth) on the other. College conservatism is illustrated in the aforementioned 1786 letter: Henry Barton complains that he does not wish to have our landmarks and fences levelled and destroyed, and even our property exposed to some hazard and uncertainty by the projects of innovators. He is sorry that the influence of Lords in our neighbourhood is likely to disturb us in our very ancient possessions, and goes on to mention one who had appropriated four acres of College woodland. (There is record too of a dispute between the Corporation and a group of landowners including John Wallop, Lord Lymington and Lord Harry Paulet over the Holy Ghost lands).

. . . . .

How long had the land been distributed in this sort of way? A cursory examination of the terriers suggest that considerable farms or holdings existed from an early date and that these passed either sold or sublet, without being broken up down to the eighteenth century, while other holdings we can see being built up over the centuries, the whole passing into fewer and fewer hands.

At the time of the Domesday survey, that is some twenty years after the Norman conquest, we have a position approaching something like equality. In the entry for Basingstoke we learn that of the twenty ploughlands, three were held by the king in demesne, and of the remaining seventeen, thirteen were held by twenty-two villeins or customary tenants and twelve cottagers, and four ploughlands held by twelve freemen or freeholders. (This includes the ploughland which was held by the Church and which was worked by two villeins and four cottagers). If 120 acres was the rough extent of a ploughland, and allowing five acres for each of the cottagers, we can say that of the local male population of 52, the freemen owned an average of forty acres each, and the twenty-two villeins an average of sixty acres each, leaving some sixty acres for the twelve cottagers. The household servants would of course, have been landless.

From 1086 we have to move on to about 1300 to glean any considerable knowledge of the Basingstoke freeholders and tenants. That current terrier gives a detailed account of the holding of William de Birteworth (formally held by Nicholas Martin) and also lists freeholds, messuages and lands purchased and rented. Also mentioned are the names of individuals holding strips adjacent to or abutting William de Birteworth. In the middlefield are mentioned the names of some 39 other land-owners. Much more work will have to be done to discover the status of these men, whether they were small peasants or perhaps bigger men who owned land in neighbouring parishes. Some of them we do know something about, for example Thomas de Worting, the Prior of Selborne. But were John de Anne, John de Hereyard and John at Hall the ancestors of William Anne, Bailiff (a big land-owner in Basingstoke in 1409), of Thomas Hereyard (who held ninety-eight acres at the same time) and of the Halls (who had built up big estates for themselves by the seventeenth century)? By the fifteenth century we do not know that William de Birteworth's lands were held by Winchester College.

From the 1543 terrier we learn that the College holding in the Basingstoke parish amounted to some 122 acres, while in 1786 the Enclosure Award gave the Warden and Scholars some 114 acres. Here is a good example of a large holding which had passed down virtually unaltered for at least five hundred years.

Another such holding which we can trace in fair detail is that of the so-called Tawkes Manor; from the inquisition of 1274 we learn that Ralph de Took was a tenant in chief and owed ten shillings in rent for a messuage and ten acres. We know from a memoranda of 1409 listing the chief owners and tenants of Basingstoke that William Tawke held twenty-nine and a half acres. He had apparently inherited John de Worting's land. (This again was a large holding which passed down intact). In the sixteenth century it was held by John Fisher of Chilton Candover and later in the seventeenth century by the Halls.

Of two other large holdings we have quite detailed histories: these are the lands of the Holy Ghost Chapel and Merton College.

The 104 acres allotted in the Enclosure Award to the Holy Ghost Chapel can be traced back intact to the sixteenth century. The Chapel itself existed before 1244 on the site of the extra-mural burial ground. Endowments like those of Michael Skylling, Lord of Lainston in 1463 were made for the purpose of having masses said for the dead. Later the Holy Ghost Guild (a social religious mutual benefit society attached to the Chapel) became in 1525 a perpetual corporation with elected wardens. Along with the other perpetual chantries, the Holy Ghost Guild was dissolved in 1550 its possessions being sold to William Warde and John Doddington for £1,675 4s. 8d. and leased to John Carter for twenty-one years. These lands were restored to the Chapel on the accession of Mary. In the charter of incorporation the restored estates were specified and included "3 acres of arable in the Northfield, 100 acres in the Common fields and two acres in Basingstoke". In the eighteenth century these lands became the subject of a dispute between the Corporation and a powerful group of land-owners. The latter accused the Corporation of obtaining Charters, lands and charities and misappropriating them, while the former claimed that these lands originally belonged to Lords Sandys and not to the crown.

The Merton College holding goes back to the end of the twelfth century. The enquiry of 1238 which listed "the lands and tenements held in Basingstoke by Walter de Merton" is printed in full in the Baigent and Millard history of the town. It is well known that with these lands he endowed the Hospital of St. John, a home for retired priests. Later, after a period as Lord Chancellor, Walter de Merton founded the Oxford College that bears his name, and in Codes of Statutes dated 1264–74 "the maintenance and encouragement of the Hospital" were given to the governing body of Merton College; later endowments can be traced from the Charters held in the treasury of Merton College. Some diminution in the size of the College holding between 1443 and 1786 is noticeable. In 1443 it amounted to some 240 acres; according to the 1578 terrier its size had fallen to 220 acres, while only 158 acres were awarded to the College by the Enclosure Award. From the late fourteenth century at least, all the College lands in Basingstoke were leased to a single tenant. In 1786 Anne Attwood was the leaseholder.

7

The Charters of Basingstoke

(Reproduced by kind permission of the *Hants & Berks Gazette*)

Among the most valuable and interesting documents in the Muniment Room at the Town Hall are the ancient Charters of the town, by which the inhabitants were made and maintained a "body corporate and politic", empowered to manage its own affairs without undue interference by outside authority. There are records of many Charters granted or confirmed to Basingstoke, for example Henry III, 1227 and 1256; Edward III, 1329; Richard II, 1392; Henry V, 1414; Henry VI, 1449; James I, 1622 and Charles I, 1641. Of these only three now exist, the remainder having doubtless perished in one of the great fires that devastated the town in medieval times, notably in 1392 and 1601. The three that survive comprise the last two, together with an Inspeximus, or contemporary official transcript of the Charter of Henry V made in 1414.

The system of Charters largely coincides with the development of local government and the de-centralised administration of local affairs that we know today. After the Norman Conquest, the whole land including the boroughs and towns was vested ultimately in the King, who parcelled it out among his followers, exacting in return certain specific services. The Lords of the Manor in turn exacted service from their tenants. The collection of the King's taxes was placed in the hands of the Sheriff or Shire-Reeve, who had to pay a fixed amount to the King's Exchequer, taking what more he could exact for himself, as was the time honoured custom of the tax-gatherer of that day. Not only were the burgesses subject to a fee farm rent legally payable to the Lord of the Manor, but they were occasionally subject to "tallage", which was an extra charge arbitrarily placed upon them by their overlords, who also sent their representatives to preside over the local Court. While considerable resentment was felt at these often illegal exactions, it was not easy to obtain redress, for it must be remembered that the so-called "towns" of these early days were of very modest size and population. As recently as 1801, Basingstoke's population only numbered 2,589. There is no local record that the town ever suffered any serious or definite setback in prosperity, so that it is safe to assume that 400 years earlier it could only be described as a mere village. It must be pictured as largely agricultural, a long straggling group of houses, stretching from the Moot Hall near the King's highway to the church among the river meadows, with a single street, the White Way, leading up to the Holy Ghost Chapel among fields across the Valley; a "town" without made streets or pavements, without drainage or water supply other than that from wells, and with its roads, apart from the high road, merely narrow lanes with ditches alongside. It must therefore be regarded as a complimentary statement rather than as a fact in the modern sense when James I describes it as "villa antiqua et populosa", an ancient and populous town. In time the agricultural interests and activities would be supplemented by those of the merchant and craftsman, and the wealth of the community would rapidly increase with the result that, on the one hand, the possessions of the traders invited the special and arbitrary attentions of the Sheriff, and on the other hand, a sense of independence would develop that keenly resented this Royal interference with business and property, with its general feeling of insecurity and its unwelcome suggestion of villenage or serfdom.

It was frequently therefore the Merchant and Craft Guilds which took the initiative in procuring from the King—often in exchange for a substantial cash payment—a Charter which would ensure to the town freedom of trading, the retention of its ancient customs and liberties, the power to elect its own officers and hold its own Courts, and to assess and collect its own taxes, and in place of the indeterminate and oppressive demands of the Sheriff to pay a fixed fee farm rent to the King's Exchequer direct. It is noteworthy that there is an invariable insistence, even by the small towns, on the confirmation of the ancient rights and usages that had pertained to them from pre-Conquest times, so that it may be said that our civil life, up to the time of the Municipal Corporations Act 1835, which established a common basis for all, had its roots in that somewhat dark period of history, the 500 years before the Norman Conquest.

The first and therefore the most important Charter of its kind, was that of Henry I to the citizens of London. It served as a model, on which was based the later Charters of Richard I to Lincoln and Winchester, and of John to Northampton, although to London alone was it granted that its citizens should be free from toil throughout the whole kingdom.

It became customary for each King, at his accession and subsequently, to confirm the Charters already existing and as he usually recited the earlier ones he added some special items of his own, which made the later documents very complex. The case of Norwich can be cited as an example. Richard II in 1378 was asked to confirm the City Charter. He began by stating that he had inspected one of Richard I, another of John, and others of 39 Henry III, 19 Edward I, 11 Edward III and 19 Edward III. Then he added his own quota, and confirmed the whole. But the Charter of 19 Edward III is found to contain one of 13 Edward I, and another of 33 Edward I while 13 Edward I contains two of 13 and 40 Henry III. As time went on matters became still worse until a Charter of Henry VII recites 24 previous Charters packed up one within another.

Neither of Basingstoke Charters is so involved, but the "Inspeximus" of Henry V gives a general idea of the way in which earlier Charters are imbedded in their successors. As it has probably never been published before, a translation of the full text is appended. It is a beautiful specimen of careful penmanship, written in Old English characters and in the usual abbreviated official Latin. As it is a transcript rather than the original Charter, it is curious to note that the large space usually occupied by an ornate initial letter has been left empty, probably from motives of economy in time, except that the appropriate small letter has been inserted in the centre. The authenticity of the document, however, is well attested by the fact that there still remains attached to it the fragments of the Great Seal of Henry V. The actual wording commences as follows:

> "Henricus dei gracia Rex Anglie et Francie et Dominus Hib'nie Omnibus ad quos presentes lre pnerunt Salutem. Inspeximus cartam Domini E. nup. Regis Angl. patri nri in nec verba. Edwardus dei gra Rex. Angl. Dominus Hibnie et Dux Aquit. Archiepis, Epis, Abbatibus, Prioribus, Comitibus, Baronibus, Justiciar, Vicecomitibus, Prepostis, Ministris et Omnibus Ballis et fidelibus suis Sal'tem . . ."

which reads:

> "HENRY, by the grace of God, King of England and France, Lord of Ireland, to all to whom these present letters shall come, Greeting. We have inspected a charter of Lord Edward our father, lately King of England in these words:
>
> EDWARD, by the grace of God, King of England, Lord of Ireland, Duke of Aquitaine, to our Archbishops, Bishops, Abbotts, Priors, Counts, Barons, Justices, Sheriffs, Provosts, Ministers, and all Bailiffs and their adherents, Greeting. We have inspected a Charter of Lord Henry our ancestor of blessed memory, one time King of England in these words:—HENRY, by the grace of God, King of England, Lord of Ireland, Duke of Normandy, and Aquitaine, Count of Anjou, to our Archbishops, Bishops, Abbotts, Priors, Counts, Barons, Justices, Sheriffs, Provosts, Ministers, and all Bailiffs and their adherents, Greeting. KNOW YE that we have granted and by this charter have confirmed to our approved men of Basingstoke our Manor of Basingstoke with the inhundred and with all other things appertaining to the farm of the said Manor to be had and held by them and their heirs, of us and our heirs, at a fee farm rent in perpetuity rendering thence every year to our Exchequer eighty pounds of sterling money, namely £40 at the Feast of St. Michael, and £40 at the Festival of Easter. RESERVING to ourselves the farm of the lands of our beloved clerk Walter de Merton which they were formally wont to render to our Exchequer for his Manor, and reserving to the said Walter and his heirs the lands and liberties which he has in the said manor. We have also granted to the same our men that they and their heirs shall, in perpetuity, have the return of writs of the Summons of our Exchequer and all other our writs appertaining to the said Manor and inhundred. Also that no Sheriff or other our Bailiff or servant shall enter the aforesaid Manor for any distraints summons or any other action except through default of the said men and their heirs. And that all men of the said Manor shall be free from toll throughout our whole realm. Also that they shall be free from road tax and from Exchequer raids in perpetuity.
>
> WHEREFORE WE desire, and have firmly resolved, for ourselves and our heirs, that the aforesaid our men in Basingstoke and their heirs shall in perpetuity have and hold well and peaceably, freely, quietly,

and wholly from us and our heirs, the aforesaid Manor of Basingstoke with all the aforesaid things and with all other liberties and customs appertaining to the farm of the said Manor. Rendering thence every year to our Exchequer £80 of sterling money, namely, £40 at the Feast of St. Michael and £40 at the Festival of Easter.

Witnesses to these things, Geoffrey de Lezinan, Gindone de Lezinan, our Priors; Richard de Grey, John de Grey, Henry de Bath, Master Simon de Wanton, Master John Mansell, Nicholas de Towers, Wankelin of Arderne, Peter Everard, Phillip de Bokeland, and others. Given under our hand at Westminster, the 20th day of May in the 40th year of our reign.

"We have inspected also a certain other Charter of the same our ancestor in these words:

HENRY, by the grace of God, King of England, Lord of Ireland, Duke of Normandy and Aquitaine, Count of Anjou, to Archbishops, Bishops, Abbotts, Priors, Counts, Barons, Justices, Sheriffs, Provosts Ministers and all Bailiffs and their adherents, Greeting. KNOW YE that we have granted and by this our Charter have confirmed to our approved men of Basingstoke that they and their heirs shall in perpetuity have this freedom namely, that neither they nor their goods shall be liable to arrest in any places whatsoever within our dominion for any debt of which the guarantors or principal debtors do not appear unless their debts are common and having the power to make satisfaction either in whole or in part they fail to do justice to their creditors and it is possible to reasonably establish this. And all men of the aforesaid Manor of Basingstoke shall be free from toll throughout our realm and dominion and shall also be free from road tax and Exchequer raids in perpetuity. WHEREFORE we desire and have firmly resolved for us and our heirs that the aforesaid men of Basingstoke and their heirs shall in perpetuity have the liberty and freedom before written as aforesaid, and we prohibit anyone under a penalty of ten pounds to in any way vex, molest or disturb them against these aforesaid liberties and freedoms.

Witness to these things, Girdone de Lezinan, Geoffrey de Lezinan, our Priors, John de Burgh, Hugh le Bigot, Henry de Bath, Master Simon de Wanton, Nicholas de Towers, William de Grey, Master John Mansell, Nicholas de St. Manro, Walkelin of Arderne, William of St. Ermina, Bartholomew de Bigot, Phillip de Bokeland and others. Given under our hand at Westminster the 29th day of May in the 40th year of our reign.

(End of Henry III Charter).

NOW WE grant and confirm the aforesaid grants and concessions, for us and our heirs, as far as in us lies, to the aforesaid our men of Basingstoke and their heirs, the men of the said town, according as the aforesaid Charters reasonably testify as they and their ancestors have hitherto held the said Manor, and have reasonably used and enjoyed the aforesaid liberties.

Witness thereto the reverend Prelates W. Archbishop of York, Primate of England, J. Elienco Bishop, H. Lincoln, Bishop, our Chancellor, Henry Duke of Lancaster, Roger de Morris, Mary Count of Marches, Thomas Wales, William de Montecute, John Mantuers, Sensechall of our Hospital, and others.

Given under our hand at Windsor the 26th day of July in the 3rd year of our reign.

(End of Edward III Charter).

NOW WE accept and approve the aforesaid concessions and grants contained in the said Charters and all and singular the grants for us and our heirs, as far as in us lies, to the men of Basingstoke and to their heirs being the men of the same town. And we grant and confirm all that the said Charters reasonably testify and as the men and their predecessors have hitherto held the said Manor and have been wont hitherto to use and reasonably enjoy the aforesaid liberties. In testimony of which we have caused these letters to be made patent. In witness myself at Westminster the 28th day of June in the second year of our reign.

(End of Inspeximus).

. . . . .

The Charters of James I, 1622 and Charles I, 1641, 200 years later deal with a situation more nearly approximating to the conditions of the present time. They introduce in great detail new forms of local government. Under the former the town is to be governed by a corporate body of the chief burgesses, who would annually elect two of their number as Bailiffs. These, with a High Steward and Under-Steward, were to act as Justices and hold a weekly Court, and to keep a prison or gaol. The weekly market was also confirmed on Wednesday. At that time the public officials included besides the Stewards and Bailiffs, a Town Clerk, an Attorney, Sergeants, Constables, a Beadle, Searchers and Sealers of leather and cloth, and an Aletaster.

This Charter was only in operation for 19 years, for in 1641 a Charter of Charles I established yet another form of government, viz., a mayor, seven aldermen and seven burgesses, with a high steward, recorder, town clerk and two sergeants-at-mace. This system continued in force until September 1835, when the present arrangement commenced.

Both documents are striking examples of decorative manuscript, the initial letters being about nine inches high, and containing within them excellent half-length pen portraits of the respective monarchs. The first lines, containing the King's territorial titles, are inscribed in ornate lettering three inches high against a background of royal leopards and conventional foliage. Both Charters consist of three or four large sheets of parchment about two feet six inches square, carefully engrossed in official Latin, but of appalling prolixity and endless repetition. In both cases the Great Seal, about six inches in diameter and in fair preservation, remains witness to the fact that the Basingstoke of those days enjoyed its corporate existence as a direct grant from the King.

The earlier document commences as follows:

> "JACOBUS dei gratia Anglie Scocie Francie et Hibnie Rex fidei defensor Omnibus ad quos presentes lre pervenerunt Salutem. Cum villa nostra de Basingstoke in Com. nostro South'ton sit villa antiqua et populosa ac probi homines ejusdem ville divers Libertates Franches, Imunitat, Exempcon, Consuet et Privileg h'uerunt . . ."

When it is remembered that the town "antiqua et populosa" was possibly as large as Kingsclere, one may well wonder what scope its inhabitants found for enjoying the varied Liberties, Franchises, Immunities, Exemptions, Customs and Privileges so carefully enumerated, but the repeated confirmation of these ancient claims, by these relatively late grants, again emphasises the tenacity and perseverance with which the English boroughs have always insisted on their right of self-determination in matters affecting their local interests and concerns.

8

The "Engagement"

(Reproduced by kind permission of the *Hants & Berks Gazette,* who published this essay in February 1924.)

A document of some historical interest and value has lately come to light in the Muniment Room at the Town Hall, viz., a contemporary record of the taking of a legal declaration of fealty to the Commonwealth, known as the "Engagement".

After the execution of Charles I in January 1649, the parliament appears to have felt its authority in the country insecure, and endeavoured to strengthen its position by obtaining a definite declaration from all men of eighteen years and upwards of their allegiance to the Commonwealth. The course of Parliamentary action necessary to secure this enactment was surprisingly varied. On 12th February, 1649, the House accepted a proposal of Ireton that all members of the Council of State should declare approval of the establishment of the High Court of Justice, the trial and execution of the King, and the abolition of the Monarchy and the House of Lords. A week later it was found that twenty-two members of the Council had refused to sign. So on 22nd February, a revised form of declaration was put forward and agreed, but this second declaration was found to be unacceptable and the order to sign it was withdrawn the next day. A third and apparently acceptable form was subsequently submitted, and on 11th October the House resolved that the "Engagement" should be taken by all members of the Council State and all members—elected and to be elected —of Parliament, extending the obligation next day to officers and men of the Army and Navy, judges and officers of the Law Courts, members of thc Inns of Court, all municipal councillors and officials, graduates and officers of the Universities, masters and scholars of Eton, Winchester and Westminster, beneficed ministers and state pensioners.

On 28th December, 1649, it was proposed that the whole population should be compelled to subscribe the "Engagement", but this was amended to "men of the age of eighteen and upwards", and on 2nd January, 1650, the Bill was carried making it compulsory on the male population to make this declaration:

> "I do declare and promise that I will be true and faithful to the Commonwealth of England as it is now established without a King or House of Lords".

The response of the people to the Act was far from universal, many refusing to take it and those who subscribed taking it only to break it. In July 1653, a Committee was set up to enquire into the facts of the case, and in January 1654, the Protector repealed the whole Act.

The Basingstoke Copy extends over a period of 18 months from 30th December 1649, to 5th August, 1651, and presents the special point of interest that the first and fullest list of names dates from 30th December, 1649, that is, only two days after the proposal to make the "Engagement" compulsory on the whole population had been put before the House, and three days before it had actually passed into law; whence it appears possible that active sympathisers with the Parliament had bestirred themselves to obtain a comprehensive expression of allegiance to the Commonwealth, even before it could be required legally. Subsequent declarations were taken from time to time and these are described as according to "the late Acte of Parliament in that behaulfe". Many of the town officers subscribed a second time in February 1650, evidently anxious to keep well within the law. But there are very few names recorded of inhabitants other than town officials, from which it may perhaps be assumed that, apart from the indefatigable few who got busy with the earlier signatures, the sympathy of the townspeople may have been largely Royalist. The constant passing and billeting of Parliamentary troops engaged at Basing House must have inflicted considerable inconvenience on the inhabitants, and they may well have felt but a qualified enthusiasm for the authority responsible.

The list of town officers is of interest in the glimpse it gives of customs and activities long since obsolete, the Court Leete and the Court Baron having given place to Sessions and County Court, while the office of Searcher and Sealer of Cloth automatically came to an end with the passing of the Basingstoke cloth industry of medieval times.

The local record is as follows:

(PAGE 1)

"The Towne Corporate of Basingstoke in the County of Southn.

I do declare and promise that I will be true and faithfull to the Common Wealthe of England as the same is nowe established without a Kinge or House of Lords.

John Aylwyn—Maior, Alderman, Justice of Peace, and one of the Comon Councellmen and Steward of some Courts Leete and Courts Baron out of the said Corporation.
James Wyther—Alderman, Justice of Peace and Comon Councellman.
Tho. South—Alderman and Comon Councellman.
Robert Stocker }
Thomas Hall } Aldermen and Comon Councellmen.
William Herne }
Edmund Pitman—Burgess and Comon Councellman.
William Clough }
John Coleman } Burgesses, Comon Councellmen and Churchwardens.
William Hawkins }
Edward Sanford—Churchwarden.
Josephus Collier—un Attorn Curie de Recordo ville p. de.
John Hunt—one of the Attornyes of the Weelely Court of Record.

Roberte Smith }
William Spyer } Overseer of the Poore, both Constables.
John Rutley—Collector for Excise.
Rob. White—Post Master.
Francis Dowse—Serieant at Mace, Minister of the Weekely Court of Record, Keeper of the Gaol or Prison there, and one of the Bailiffs of the Mannor and Hundred of Basingstoke aforesaid.
Richard Whittier—the other Serieant att Mace and Minister of the said Weekely Court and the other Bailiff of the said Mannor and Hundred.

(PAGE 2)

Rob. Ramford—Schoolemaster of the pettye Schoole.
Hugh White }
Rich. Butler } Overseers of the Poore.
Peter Sainsbere—Clerke.
Richard Hall—horse post.
The mke of Richard Lewis—horse post.
The mke of Thomas Bateman—one of the Tythingemen.
The mke of Benjamin Dycey—th'other Tythingeman.
The mke of Robert Cater }
The mke of Wm. Warner, th'elder } Searchers and Sealers for Cloth.

The officers and ministers hereabove named uppon the Thirtieth Daye of December Anno Dni 1649 att the said Towne of Basingstoke did subscribe the said Engagement as is above menconed before us the Maior and Justices of Peace of the same Towne whose names are hereunder written.

(PAGE 3)

The Towne Corporate, etc.
I doe declare, etc.:
Jo. Aylwyn—Maior, Justice of Peace, Alderman and Comon Councellman.
James Wither—Justice of Peace, Alderman and Comon Councellman.
Tho. South—Sen. Alderman.
Thomas Hall—Alderman.
Edmond Pittman—Burgesse.
William Clough—Burgesse.
William Hawkins—Burgesse.
Ro. Pococke—Schoolemaster of the Free Schoole.
Laur. Pococke—Usher of the same Schoole.
John Hunt—one of the Attornyes of the Weekely Court of Record.
John Rutley—Collector for Excise.
Robert Ramford—Schoolemaster of the Pettye Schoole.
Paul Wheeler—Towne Clerke.
Robert Smith }
William Spier } Constables.
The mke of Thomas Bateman—Tythingman.

The Engagement here above menconed was given and administered unto and was taken and subscribed by the officers and p'sons here before named resideinge within the said Towne Corporate of Basingstoke aforesaid the Nyneteenthe daye of February Anno Dni 1649 by and before John Aylwyn, gent., Maior of the said Towne, and James Wither, gent., twoe of the Justices of Peace of the same Towne accordinge to the late Acte of Parliament in that behaulfe.

Jo. Aylwyn, Maior, James Wither.

(PAGE 4)

The mke of Richard Woodrofe—Burgesse.
John Coleman—Burgesse.
William Elliott—one of the Attorneyes of the Weekely Court of Record there and Deputy Steward of the Courte Leete and Court Baron of the Mannor of Basingstoke for the p'sent.
Francis Dowse, Richard Whittier } Sergeants at Mace, Ministers of the Weekely Courte of Record, and Bailiffs of the Mannor and Hundred of Basingstoke aforesaid.
Peter Sainsbere—Parishe Clerke.
Richard Hall—horse post.

And also the Engagement aforesaid was given and administered unto and was taken and subscribed by the other Officers and p'sons lastly here above named resideinge as aforesaid the twentieth daye of February aforesaid in the said yeare 1649 by and before us the said Maior and Justices of Peace here above named accordinge to the Acte of Parliament aforesaid.

Jo. Aylwyn, Maior, James Wither.

The Towne Corporate, etc.
I doe declare, etc.:
19 Aprilis 1650—John Davis, clothier, of the age of eighteene yeares and upwards.
20 Aprilis 1650—Richard Spittle, inholder.
22 Aprilis 1650—The mke of George Edwards, blackesmith.
4 May 1650—Steph. Mayne.

The persons here above named Inhabitants of the said Towne of the sevall dayes against their names respectively did there take and subscribe the said Engagement in the manner and forme abovesaid accordinge to the late Acte of Parliament in that behaulfe before us twoe of the Justices of Peace of the said Towne whose names are hereunder written.

John Aylwyn, Maior, James Wyther.
IIII. May 1650.

(PAGE 5)

The Town Corporate, etc.
I doe declare, etc.
8 May 1650—Thomas Denham.

8 May 1650—The mke of Johan Blunden Wydowe.
8 May 1650—Robert Stocker.
8 May 1650—William Herne.
5 June 1650—William Blunden.

The p'sons above named inhabitants etc. 5 June 1650.

The 5th day of August, 1651.

William Warner of the said Towne of Basingstoke, clothier, did then and there take the said Engagement (to wit), I doe declare, etc., before us two of the Justices of Peace of the said Towne whose names are hereunder written.

Will Warner.

Jo. Aylwyn,
Tho. South."

(Following the publication of this article, a letter to the Editor was printed from Reginald F. Bigg-Wither of Hartley Wintney, pointing out that the James Wyther, or Wither referred to in the "Engagement" was the younger brother of the poet George Wither. He was afterwards Mayor of Basingstoke. The two brothers were grandsons of Richard Wither, of Manydown, who died in 1577.)

XVI Church Street Methodist Church (prior to its demolition for Town Development), in 1964

XVII The Engineers Arms, Reading Road, just before demolition in 1966

XVIII The 'Bus Station, off Wote Street, prior to the construction of the present modern Station, about 1960

XIX A typical scene at the cattle market in 1960

XX Danes Corner, Wote Street, once the home of Dr. Andrews, who, like George Willis was most interested in local history

XXI Hackwood Road, before the Toll House was demolished. This was the site of one of the many toll gates in the area (Toll House was demolished in 1929)

XXII Brambly's Lane, about 1905, "in the country". (Looking southward, with Winchester Road in the far background)

9

The Basingstoke Canal

At about the same time as the Parliamentary Commissioners for enclosure were at work, other individuals were working on a scheme which was to bring further change in the appearance and character of the town. A proposal to link Basingstoke to the Thames via a canal and the River Wey was put forward as early as 1769, and in 1770, a meeting about the proposal was held in the Town Hall, Basingstoke. At this meeting it was "resolved that the making of a navigable canal from Basingstoke to communicate with the River Thames at a place called Monkey Island, near Windsor, will be of great public utility".

The canal was intended as a route from London to Salisbury and the west of England, alternative to that via Reading, Newbury and the River Kennet.

The Rev. S. Shaw, writing of his journey to the west of England in 1788 pointed out the probable advantages of the proposed new canal: a reduction in the costs of conveying goods to and from London, easier transport of chalk for use in improving the heathlands of Surrey.

In 1778 the Company of Proprietors of the Basingstoke Canal Navigation was formed. The Parliamentary reference was as follows:

> "An Act for making a navigable canal from the town of Basingstoke, to communicate with the river Wey in the parish of Chertsey, County Surrey, and to the south east side of the turnpike road in the parish of Turgiss, County of Southampton.
>
> 18 Geo. III."

Included among the proprietors of the newly-formed company were the Earl of Northington, the Earl of Portsmouth, General Grant and Joseph Portal. The Mayor of Basingstoke was a member by virtue of his office. The Corporation was a contributor to the funds of the company "from a belief that the canal would benefit the town". Between 1782 and 1805 the Corporation invested £700. Other proprietors included such locally well-known names as thc Rcv. T. Sheppard, John Covey and Thomas May junior. The original capital was £126,000 raised in £100 shares, after expending this the Company borrowed £32,000 to complete the works.

In 1793 the plan was given the official go-ahead in these words:

> "An Act for effectually carrying into execution an Act of Parliament of the 18 Geo. III for making a navigable canal from the town of Basingstoke to communicate with the River Wey in the parish of Chertsey . . . 33 Geo. III."

Construction was begun some time after this date and the canal was open for traffic to Basingstoke in 1796. It was not as commercially successful as had been anticipated and the reasons for this must be sought in changed economic and political circumstances. In the first place, the Kennet and Avon Canal, which was opened throughout its route in 1810, proved to be too strong a rival, with its better access to the west country. A second factor was the ending of the Napoleonic Wars, which meant it was once again safe for coasting vessels to use ports along the Channel coast, thus making it unnecessary for goods in transit to Portsmouth and Southampton to make use of the canal. On 21st October, 1816, it was realised by the Canal Company "that from the facilities afforded in peace to the conveyance of goods by sea, some considerable injury must be sustained by the canal". Previously, around 1802, it had been stated that "a considerable quantity of the goods conveyed to the Isle of Wight, Jersey, Guernsey, etc. which used to go up the canal to Basingstoke and thence by wagon to Southampton are now sent directly from the Thames by vessels trading to those islands".

There had been a proposal for the Basingstoke Canal to be linked from Basing to Newbury and thus to the Kennet and Avon Canal, by a Hants and Berks Junction Canal. This proposal was put before Parliament in 1825 but failed to gain the necessary sanction. The bulk of the opposition to this scheme, which might have had some effect on the trade of the Thames downstream from Reading, came from the Thames Commissioners. In a speech on behalf of its clients, counsel poured scorn on the prospects of such a scheme, saying of the Basingstoke Canal: "The concern has long been bankrupt, its dividends as they always have been, naught. There is but one last lingering trader upon it, and he is on the point of flitting lest his ruin should be consummated. From what quarter can a single ray of hope be expected to break in upon a scene of such utter desolation?". The answer was that there did seem to be little hope, for there was already appearing a hint of stronger competition to come. On 22nd September, 1831, a meeting of the company was held "to adopt such measures as may be necessary for the interests of this Company, in regard to the proposed Railway from London to Southampton".

The failure of the canal's traffic to come up to expectations is shown by figures of tonnage carried and net revenue earned:

1799–1800	17,877 tons	£1,345
1800–1801	18,638 tons	£3,038
1801–1802	18,816 tons	£1,925

Ironically, one of the busiest years for the canal was 1836, when it carried materials for the building of the railways and thus it contributed to its own eventual decline. In November 1840 a notice appeared in the *Hampshire Chronicle* about the payment of dividends by the Basingstoke Canal Navigation. The notice stated that dividends at 2 per cent would be payable for the year 1835; it also added that shareholders who had not received dividends for the years 1824 to 1834 could now receive them.

It would be incorrect to say the canal did not perform a useful function in the economic life of the town and its neighbourhood. It was essentially an agricultural canal, serving a mainly rural area and therefore could not be expected to have the volume of traffic of the industrial canals of the north. The important commodities carried on our canal were the farming produce of the region, including malt, which was one of the chief manufactures of the town, manure and also chalk for use in improving the heathlands of the country lying to the east of the town. A contemporary account stresses the importance of the canal for "the fetching of coals, which may come from the port of London or from some of those places on the Thames where Midland coal is brought for sale, cheaper than the sea-borne coal from London, but inferior in quality for domestic purposes". The writer of this account, having discussed the possibility of carrying the line of the canal further westward to link up with the Test, comes to the conclusion that Basingstoke does not suffer from being the terminus of the canal "because if thereby becomes a place at which the canal-borne goods, both to and from the metropolis are stored, and this gives a good deal of bustle and employment and consequent profit to the inhabitants". There were at the Wharf depots, for coal and other commodities. The Wharf site was sometimes used for a market. Twice in 1840 a cheese market was held there. At the first of these, held in June, there was a considerable attendance of dealers, and about 250 tons of cheese, a large proportion of superior quality, was displayed for sale. The account of the event pointed out the advantage of having the market so near the railway and canal and also the advantage of freedom from paying any toll. A similar market was held in November of the same year; this was also well attended by dealers from London and elsewhere.

Records in the possession of the oldest manufacturing firm in the town, Wallis and Steevens Ltd., show a good indication of the cargoes carried and other incidental information. (This is reproduced by kind permission of Wallis and Steevens Ltd.) In 1844 the cargoes carried were varied: lead, coal and metal; nails, ironmongery and glass; oil, grease, candles and blacking; vinegar, rum, yarn and rags; pork and bacon; flour, oats, loaves, cheese, butter and sugar. By 1849, however the last entries in the book listed only seven commodities carried: pipe oil, lead, coal, beans, wheat, soap and rags.

These records also show that only a few barges used the canal between the years of 1844 and 1849; the *Dwarf*, the *Wasp*, and the *Britannia* made one journey each, the *Harriet* and the *Alresford* a few more, but the most frequently seen barges during this period were the *Independent*, the *Defiant*, the *Dolphin* and the *Dispatch*. The last two recorded journeys on the canal were made at the end of February 1849, by the *Independent* and the *Dolphin* who carried 56 tons and 58 tons respectively. The *Independent's* fee of 56s. does not appear to have been settled, and although the *Dolphin* paid £5, it appears that two items of 14s. and 28s. were not settled.

10

The Nineteenth Century: Re-organisation and Changes

In the attempt to reconstruct the character of the economic life of the town in the early part of the nineteenth century, there is little to draw upon apart from the descriptive detail included in directories of the period.

From an examination of a list of trades carried on in the town (given in the *Hampshire Directory* of 1784) it is apparent that Basingstoke was then no different from the majority of small market towns remote from those areas which were undergoing rapid growth as a result of proximity to coal. It was then a small town with a population of less than 2,500, serving for most purposes a very limited and thinly populated hinterland. Its main function was to provide markets for the farmers of the district (that is, farms within Basingstoke). As such, it provided the traditional crafts and trades associated with such an economy (for example, May's brewery from 1750 onwards).

Basingstoke was "a large populous town, with a great market for all sorts of corn, especially here being great trade in malt, as there is in druggets, shalloons, etc." so wrote the author of "Collections for the History of Hampshire and the Bishopric of Winchester" in 1795.

The directory of 1804 was non-committal about the relative importance of the woollen trade but did say that the business of malting was carried on to a considerable extent and employed a great number of persons. The directory of 1828 was more definite about the decline in importance of the woollen trade, adding the comment that "the trade in corn and malt is considerable (much improved by the canal) and upon the Loddon stream are several flour mills".

The picture had not substantially altered by 1837, when the Commissioners for Municipal Corporations' Boundaries said of the town: "It is represented to be gradually increasing in size and importance. It contains no manufactories, but is a place of very great thoroughfare and is situated in the centre of a rich agricultural district. The markets held here are well attended, being resorted to by persons from Andover, Winchester, Newbury and Reading".

The Parliamentary Gazetteer for 1847, commenting that in 1821, of the 365 families returned as engaged in various trades or manufactures, the majority were employed in making druggets and shalloons, recorded that this manufacture had "declined considerably of late years". At this time the main business was the trade in corn and malt. The situation of the town at the centre of a network of roads and on a canal linking it to London undoubtedly played a great part in widening the economic sphere of influence of the town.

Three years after the Commissioners for Municipal Corporations' Boundaries reported on the "state of the town" the railway link with London and Southampton had been completed. This was to be the most important contributor to the extension of the area served by the town, so essential for its growth in the second half of the century. The transition from market town to manufacturing centre was however to be a very gradual one.

It was at this time that Parliament, having passed the 1832 Reform Bill which reorganised constituencies and set in motion changes in the form and character of central government, turned its attention to local government by initiating a review of municipal corporation.

In common with other boroughs, Basingstoke came under the scrutiny of members of the Commission for Municipal Corporations some time in 1834. These gentlemen reported on the main aspects of their enquiry in 1835. Their first concern was with the machinery of local government in the town. They found that this was in a form unchanged since the time of Charles I, who in 1641 had given the town a Charter to replace the one granted by James I in 1622. As has already been shown in an earlier essay the 1641 Charter authorised the town to have a Corporation consisting of a mayor, seven aldermen and seven burgesses, the mayor being elected annually from among the aldermen. The aldermen were chosen from among "the seven burgesses, who in turn were elected from among the inhabitant householders of the borough" by the mayor, aldermen and burgesses.

As in most other boroughs at the time the Commission reported the members of the Corporation came from a small section of the population. The movement for reform reorganised the abuses and dangers inherent in a form of government which, by encouraging self-perpetuation and nepotism, could hardly be representative of the interests of all the inhabitants of the growing town, and might easily fail to meet the demands of the changing times.

The lack of representation was perhaps more serious in the towns of the rapidly industrialising north than in the small market towns of the south but even in Basingstoke the Commissioners drew attention to the fact that some members of the Corporation were related.

In the conclusion to their report, they stated:

> "The corporate officers are objects of ambition to the respectable inhabitants, who are desirous to have the power of electing their own officers. It is felt to be a grievance that the corporation allow non-residents to remain members of their body, and that they have elected strangers to fill up the vacancies in the corporation to the neglect of the native inhabitants of the town. In all other respects the conduct of the corporation both as to the management of their affairs and as to the administration of justice has deserved the confidence of the inhabitants."

It is true that an earlier part of the report mentions that the accounts of the town had not been kept with regularity up to 1805, but that since then they had been "attended to with more care" being kept by a chamberlain, a member of the corporation who was paid a salary of £25 a year.

Much more detail is given in the report; there is for example, reference to the various prices of legislation by which changes in the appearances and economic life of the town were being changed. Mention is also made of the many charities in the town, for which the corporation were trustees.

The Municipal Reform Act, which was to bring about the changes thought desirable, was passed by Parliament on 9th September, 1835, and on 26th December in the same year, the first new councillors for Basingstoke were elected, the election of aldermen and Mayor taking place three days later. Although its size has increased and its powers have undergone continual evolution, the form of the corporation then established has persisted to the present day.

The members of the Corporation of Basingstoke, when the Commission reported were as follows:

Aldermen—Thomas May (common brewer), Robert Hulbert, Snr., Esq., Charles May, Snr. (common brewer), Charles Hawthorn, Esq., James Warne (attorney at law), William Anthony Lewis (attorney at law), John Simmons (banker), Richard Eyles, Esq. Of these James Warne was Mayor at the time.

Burgesses—Charles May, Jnr. (common brewer), Thomas Workman (surgeon), Charles Headeach (gentleman), Robert Hulbert, Jnr. (chemist), John Osmond Nicholls (surgeon), and John Sansom (schoolmaster). The Commissioners drew attention to the fact that Messrs. May were related, also Messrs. Hulbert, also Mr. Headeach to Mr. Workman.

The members of the new council after the Municipal Reform Act 1835.

Elected Councillors (election 26th December 1835)—John Simmons, Thomas May, James Warne, Charles May, Jnr., Charles Lyford, Edward Covey, Thomas Workman, Robert Cottle, Robert Skeat Hulbert, George Paice, Charles Simmons and William Houghton.

Elected Aldermen (29th December, 1835)—John Simmons, Thomas May, Charles Lyford and Robert Cottle.

Elected Mayor—John Simmons.

Town Clerk—William Anthony Lewis.

A second election took place on 9th January 1836, when five more councillors were elected: George Lamb (Solicitor), Henry Brownjohn (Wine merchant), Robert Curtis (Coach proprietor), Edward Penton (maltster) and George Caston (ironmonger).

Treasurer—Charles Headeach.

Sergeants-at-Mace—James Cooper and Charles Cox, Jnr.

Amusing though it may seem to us who have the advantage of hindsight, the Commissioners considered that a reduction in the area of the borough was necessary: "On all sides but the north-east, the boundaries reach between one and two miles from the town. On the latter side, the parish boundary is at such a distance from the town that it may conveniently be retained for the future boundary of the borough. On the other sides, however, the present limits are *much too extensive* for municipal purposes." The report went on to detail the proposed boundaries; these were thought "to allow sufficient space for whatever extension of the town may take place along any of the high roads".

Another part of the report is interesting for the contribution it makes to our understanding of the social conditions of the times. It is stated that the number of houses in the borough increased from 266 in 1831 to 352 in 1835; it is further stated however, that 100 houses in the borough were not rated because of the poverty of their inhabitants.

. . . . .

The physical appearance of the town and its neighbourhood began to change at the end of the eighteenth century; the enclosure of the open fields, which had been a feature of the town for hundreds of years and the cutting of the canal were perhaps the most striking changes that had occurred.

The nineteenth century brought more change. In 1832, on 20th May, the "taking down" of the old Town Hall began. It was replaced by a building on almost the same site on the north side of the market place, which was itself enlarged under powers obtained under an Act of 1829:

> "10. Geo. IV. An Act for enlarging the Market Place in the Town of Basingstoke, in the County of Southampton, and for fixing and regulating the markets of the said town and for establishing a market for live cattle adjoining the same."

The new building was erected on the site of two shops (one belonging to Mr. Caston) and the Royal Oak Inn. In the diary of Samuel Attwood, we have an account of the laying of the first stone on 8th June:

> "The first stone of the new Town Hall was laid with great ceremony by J. Simmons, Esq., Mayor, attended by the Corporation, several gentry, the Bard, and a large concourse of spectators—a new sovereign, crown piece, penny, halfpenny and a farthing were deposited in the new stone, all new coins of King William."

The new building, which cost in all nearly £10,000 stood on pillars, leaving an open space below, which provided shelter for people attending the market. (There were later some alterations made.)

Throughout the early part of the century, it was the scene of activities as varied as meetings of the North Hampshire Agricultural Society, lectures to the Mechanics' Institute, and the Easter County Balls, which were such a feature of the social scene. One of these, in April 1841, was attended by a "numerous and fashionable company" which included Lord and Lady Bolton, Lord Worsley, M.P., Mr. Chute, M.P., and Mrs. Chute, Lady Rycroft, Lady Wilder, and Mrs. St. John and family. We are told that "dancing commenced at 10 o'clock, and continued with untiring spirit to Targett's celebrated Quadrille Band, which exerted itself with unequalled effect until long past dawn on Friday. The polite attention of the stewards was unremitting and this joined to the arrangements of Mr. Klitz considerably enhanced the pleasures of an evening unusually brilliant and attractive". The other occasion when the Town Hall was made use of in this way was the concluding day of Basingstoke Races.

At no great distance from the Market Place, two new buildings had gone up at the very beginning of the century. The first of these was the new church for the Congregationalists. Congregationalists had played an active part in the religious life of the town, despite the many difficulties placed in their way. The year 1663 had seen the beginnings of Congregationalism in Basingstoke, when John Hook, ejected from his living as a priest of the Church of England, as were so many others, continued his ministry among the people of Basingstoke until 1695 (when the Toleration Act was passed), by holding religious meetings in people's houses. After the Act was passed, the Congregationalists opened their first meeting-house in Cross Street, next to the Blue Coat School. Towards the end of the eighteenth century members of the Independent Meeting House decided that they needed a larger building, because of their increasing membership. Their decision led to the opening (in May 1800) of the Meeting House which we know today as the London Street Congregational Church.

The other new building at that time was also a church. It was opened in Wote Street in 1802 for members of the Countess of Huntingdon's Connexion, a church which originated from the conversion to Methodism of Selina, Countess of Huntingdon in 1739. One of her original aims was to convert her friends and acquaintances in the upper classes to the ideas and beliefs of Wesley and Whitefield. It was for this reason that most of her original foundations of churches, mainly during the period 1761–79 took place in the fashionable centres, such as spas like Bath, Tunbridge Wells and Worcester.

In 1834, the town welcomed the opening of the gasworks on the east side of a lane which came to be known as Gashouse Lane. As Samuel Attwood records in his diary for 1st October 1834: "A partial illumination two nights—the Bard painted the Town—public dinners, suppers—bells ringing on the occasion." The decision to establish a company for the supply of "inflammable air" was taken at a meeting held on 19th December, 1833. The meeting was covered by Mr. George Carton, ironmonger; Mr. Barlow, a gas engineer from the Staines and Egham gasworks was present. It is perhaps significant that the contract for the works of laying the mains and service pipes to local tradesmen was given to T. Barlow and Sons. Originally there were 150 consumers and there were in addition a few public lamps. It is recorded in the history of the Company that consumption increased with the coming of the L. & S.W. Railway, and also with the increasing appreciation of the value of gas as a means of illumination. Contributing to this would be talks, such as that given to the Mechanics' Institute in December, 1841 by Mr. Sharp of Winchester on "Principle and Practice of cooking by gas".

The coming of the railway in 1839 caused further changes in the shape of the town and the neighbourhood. The building of the great embankment across the Loddon, the cutting through the chalk at the eastern approach to the town, the building of the station, and then in 1848 the opening of the second station, for the Great Western Railway, immediately to the north of the L. & S.W.R. station—all these left their mark on the town.

The year 1865 was also important for an addition to the townscape. On 1st March, 1865, the new Corn Exchange was opened for business. It was to celebrate this event that about 340 gentlemen, farmers and tradesmen dined together on 22nd February. Lord Bolton led the festivities. We are told that "his Lordship was exorted into the town by about 100 tenents, tradesmen and friends preceded by the Basingstoke Band, with bells ringing and other demonstrations of joy. To wind up the affair a ball took place the same night in the Town Hall, which closed about four the next morning. Mrs. Daniels of the Red Lion provided the dinner etc. to both parties". The opening of the Corn Exchange is a reminder to us of the dependence of the town on the health of the farming round about. The population, according to the 1801 census had been 2,589, but by 1837 it was approaching 4,000 and about 1,000 more by the time the Corn Exchange was opened.

The next major change in the town was in 1869, when, on 13th October the Mechanics' Institute gained a building of their own in New Street. It was called the Mechanics' Institute and Club, and the opening ceremony was performed by Canon Charles Kingsley, the Rector of Eversley, perhaps better known as the author of "The Water Babies".

The idea of providing instruction for members of the working classes originated in Glasgow. It is with this development that we particularly associate the name of Birkbeck. When Birkbeck moved to London in 1804, the men who had been his students in Glasgow formed themselves into what they called a "Mechanics' Institute", their object being to instruct artisans "in the scientific principles of arts and manufactures". Birkbeck set up an institute in London in 1823 and by 1850 there were 610 of these throughout the country.

The Basingstoke Institute was founded on 28th March 1841. The inaugural address was given by Mr. C. E. Lefroy, who, wishing to point out the value of leisure time, chose a Biblical text on his theme: "The night cometh when no man can work". In the nineteenth century, this was not generally true, for the majority of workers, whether in factory or on the land, had neither the leisure nor the money to spare for such pursuits. It is perhaps not surprising, therefore that the membership of the institutes were not exactly as had originally been intended by Birkbeck and his followers. The text of the address was printed and published by Mr. Robert Cottle, with the intention of devoting all the proceeds to "the purchase of some useful philosophical apparatus to be presented to the institution".

In the following month the Institute held its first lecture. Mr. Carter of Flaxfield House was the lecturer and the subject was "Arithmetic". It was "numerously and respectably attended" by an audience, which, far from finding the talk dry and uninteresting, listened attentively to an account of the history of numbers, and frequently applauded the lecturer for his mastery of the subject.

Among other topics which were the subject of lectures during the year of foundation were:

1. The Philosophy of Memory—Mr. Pearsall of Andover.
2. Mental culture as a means of combating social backwardness and political despotism—Mr. White of Reading.

3. The Mechanical Properties of Steam—Mr. Burt of Southampton.
4. The Sensible Motion of Bodies—Mr. Lefroy of Basingstoke.
5. The Conflict between Religion and Science—the Rev. Bigg-Wither of Basingstoke.
6. Ornithology—Mr. Mudie of Portsmouth.
7. The Principle and Practice of cooking by Gas—Mr. Sharp of Winchester.

. . . . .

Between 1871 and 1881 the population of the town increased from 5,574 to 6,681. During this time, particularly in the latter half of the decade, the main theme in the life of the town was its growth and the need to provide housing and improved amenities for an increasing population. New houses were necessary and more important still the provision of a safe piped water supply and sewerage system was becoming of vital importance.

The town had begun to expand westwards along the Loddon Valley in the area known as Longcroft (later to be known as Newtown). Despite the housing provided in this "a growing suburb of the town" there were complaints of a scarcity of houses for working people.

In 1878, in connection with the sale of some land to the north of the Great Western Railway station, reference was made to building 50–100 working men's cottages at a rental of £10–£12 a year each, "that are so needed about the town".

In 1879 it was stated that accommodation was nowhere equal to the demand for it and that a builder laying the foundation for a house immediately received an application for it. The new neighbourhood in Newtown was said to be growing up but not fast enough. The example was quoted of one agent "who scarcely ever had a cottage change hands, but that he had 18 names on his books, should one become vacant". This shortage of housing in a town which was otherwise growing and becoming prosperous, was blamed on the reluctance of the corporation to permit the building of cottages. This view is well put in a letter to the local paper of 15th February, 1879, about the state of Longcroft Road: "if the authorities wish to discourage private enterprise in meeting what is admitted to be one of the town's sorest needs, viz., the creation of cottages for the largely increased number of its working population, they cannot do better than pursue the course they are doing". After a reference to an apparent unwillingness to allow working men to settle down among the select population of Basingstoke, the letter concluded "such a course", it is easily seen, must be fraught with evil consequences for the prosperity of the town".

Another problem facing the corporation was that of providing proper roads and of lighting them adequately. All these improvements had to be paid for and it is therefore not surprising that the question of the inequity of rates became a very lively one. A letter from Mr. R. Wallis of Eastlands, contains some very interesting figures, showing the rateable value of many properties in the town. He points out that these were obtained from the official record. The topic was to come more to the fore when measures to improve the sanitation of the town came under discussion.

That improvements were necessary was shown by a report made in 1871 to the Local Government Board by Dr. Ballard. He had drawn attention to the shortcomings of the authorities in the following words: "There are two Local Sanitary Authorities—one of which does nothing and the other next to nothing, except by spurts. The Paving and Lighting Commissioners do nothing to amend the drainage of the town because they cannot raise the necessary funds for the purpose; and so every man drains his own premises exactly as is most convenient to himself without any regard to the health or convenience of his neighbours".

While problems of housing and sanitation were directly occupying of the members of the corporation and indirectly the citizens of Basingstoke, there was renewed discussion of the proposal by the L. & S.W. Railway to build a carriage works in the town. It would seem that the scheme "so manifestly advantageous to the town" was opposed by members of the corporation. Their opposition was attributed to a belief that such works would bring a class of people to the town that would lower its reputation. It was argued that, far from discouraging development such as this, the council should be active in encouraging any proposal calculated to promote the well-being of the town. In 1879, the same theme was continued in a letter to the local paper, under the heading "Look Ahead Basingstoke":

> "Had it not been for some of them" (the men in authority) "we should have the fields between here and Worting covered with houses and railway works, but they, as now, could not see an inch before their eyes, and, for fear of the gross immorality that would be introduced into the quiet town of Basingstoke, they opposed in every way the now powerful S.W. Railway Company having any works here, and to this day the Company have never forgotten it".

The fact was that eventually the carriage works were established, not at Basingstoke but at Bishopstoke (Eastleigh).

As we have seen much use was made of the local newspaper for letters about local affairs. It was only from 1878 that the town had the means of carrying on public discussion affecting the life of the town. In that year the first edition of the *Hants and Berks Gazette* (now known as the *Basingstoke Gazette*) appeared in January. Early in the life of the paper, the editor found it necessary to adminster a tactful rebuke to a certain correspondent: "Constant reader, has, we think, aired his opinions sufficiently on the subject of his special grievance".

We must now revert to the question of the sewerage scheme for the town. Early in 1878, there appeared a reference in the local paper to the acceptance of tenders to carry out the drainage scheme "within the next nine months". Two firms were mentioned, Small of Gloucester and Hookway of Bideford. There was opposition to the scheme on the grounds of cost. It was thought to be too heavy a burden, particularly on the smaller rate-payer: "is there no spirit in this old town to agitate against this enormous outlay, ere it be too late?".

. . . . .

The economy of the town still continued to be closely related to the farming of the country round about, that is, farms within the borough.

The town continued to serve the countryside as it had done in the past but changes were occuring, and as far as farming was concerned, some of these changes reflected what was happening to British farming as a whole. Disenchantment set in—locally the end of the farming hey-day, the decrease of arable and increase of permanent pasture, the decline in numbers employed; the fall in agricultural wages and the depopulation of the countryside.

The town continued to hold fairs. In 1887 a sheep fair was held on 13th July, most likely at Fairfields; on this day 3,500 sheep and lambs were penned. During the same year, when discussions were going on about the management of fairs and markets, it was reported that the number of pennings had fallen off, because of the increase in the number of regular weekly auction sales. These it was stated, were held in nearly every market town.

The Michaelmas fair was held on 11th and 12th October in the same year, there, changing times and circumstances could certainly be noticed. Traditionally the Michaelmas fair was a hiring fair, the occasion when farm workers, in search of a new situation, appeared wearing in their hats an indication of their particular calling. A carter would have worn a piece of plaited whipcord, a shepherd a tuft of wool, a cowman hairs from a cow's tail, and a ploughman straw. It would seem that by 1887 the old system of hiring was gradually dying out, becoming almost completely replaced by the advertisement of jobs in the newspaper. As a result only a small number of farm-workers came into the town expressly for the purpose of being hired. They did come however, for making purchases and for enjoying themselves, for the fair was also a pleasure fair; in the evening particularly, country and townspeople mingled on the fairground, enjoying themselves among the roundabouts, swinging boats, coconut shies, shooting galleries and sideshows of all kinds. Although a large number of visitors came in from the country, they caused little trouble. Many of them showed "a fondness for John Barleycorn" but "drunken-ness was confined to a few, but this few did not reach the advanced stage. The number of street quarrels was likewise very small".

It was customary for the shopkeepers of the town to take advantage of this rural influx by holding Michaelmas sales. At this time the local paper would contain such advertisements as "Michaelmas clothing". The report of the 1887 fair referred to the fall in agricultural wages and said that this had a considerable influence on the trade of the town: "Complaints of the want of ready-money purchases are general". The account concluded by saying that the farmer himself was feeling the pinch of hard times and therefore could hardly be expected to pay more for his labour.

One of the firms to advertise sales of Michaelmas clothing was that of Thomas Burberry. Mr. Burberry established his business in the town some years before 1878 "without signs of pretentious demonstration, he prudently secured premises in Winchester Street, eminently suitable and capable of great extension". The business prospered and additions did have to be made. Eventually the general manufacturing side of the trade was transferred to Messrs. Gerrish, Ames and Simpkins, for whom a new factory was opened on Station Hill in 1878.

The weekly markets continued to be held, to serve the needs of the townspeople and country people alike, and there were in addition special auction markets from time to time, not only for stock and grain but also for wool. At Messrs. Raynbird's sale in July 1909 "a good competition was experienced, every lot changing hands". The company coming from the main towns of the West Riding, from Leicester, Winchester, Reading and also from Scotland and Ireland. In 1911 the July sale of Messrs. Raynbird disposed of 18,000 fleeces. Smaller quantities were offered by Messsrs. Gillman and Sollom; in 1911 2,500 fleeces went to "buyers from all parts" at prices which were lower than in the previous year.

Given the appropriate occasion, the townspeople could give themselves over to enjoying themselves to the full. Such an occasion came in 1887 with the Jubilee of Queen Victoria. The celebrations, processions, illuminations, feasting and sports took place over two days. On the first day there was a procession of children from the Sunday Schools in the town. The music was provided by the band of "K" Company of the 1st Hampshire Rifle Volunteers, and his Worship the Mayor, John May, was on horseback for the occasion. After the procession there was tea for the children at tables outside the Town Hall. The day was rounded off with games and sports on the Common, at the end of which the Mayor called for three hearty cheers for the Queen.

The second day (which was a Tuesday) was somewhat similar except that it was the turn of the grown-ups. The day began with the Mayor's breakfast for the members of the Council and Borough Officials. The adults too had their procession; all branches of civic life were represented in a perambulation of the town which lasted about three quarters of an hour, ending just before noon. The festival dinner, at which there were no less than 2,500 diners, was eaten at tables set out along London Street and Winchester Street. The day ended, as the previous one, with sports and games on the Common.

John May, who was in his third year of office as Mayor, came from a family which had long since been associated with the town. A May had been a member of the Guild of the Holy Ghost in 1557; another had been Mayor in 1711; others had also served the town in the same capacity. One of these, Thomas May, Junior, the son of the founder of the firm of brewers, maltsters and farmers was Mayor ten times. The firm was established in 1750 in Brook Street, where it had both its brewery and one of its farms, Glebe Farm.

John May was the holder of the office of Mayor in three subsequent years, 1893–94, 1896–97, and 1901–02. Two of these years of office were also occasions of great national importance, the first being the Diamond Jubilee of Queen Victoria, the other being the Coronation of King Edward VII. On both these occasions as on the previous one in 1887, he contributed generously to the costs of the celebrations. His generosity took many other forms; he is remembered for his purchase of The Folly for use as a cricket ground (he was himself an enthusiastic cricketer); he provided at his own expense, a drill hall for "K" Company of the 1st Hampshire Rifle Volunteers, in which he himself served from 1859 to 1898, latterly as Lt.-Col. The Drill Hall later became the Plaza Cinema. He was also a benefactor of the Hospital, providing the money for one wing of the building. The clock tower, which for many years graced the Town Hall was another of John May's gifts to the town, this was to commemorate Queen Victoria's Golden Jubilee. He also gave Basingstoke the Band Stand which now is in the War Memorial Park, but which used to be in Fairfields Recreation Ground. The set of nine bells, which were placed in All Saints' Church when it was erected were yet another gift to the town. He died in 1920. The firm of which he was chairman for so long, went into voluntary liquidation in 1950, but the name of May still lives on in May Street, close to the site of the old brewery and farm. This road was formerly called Longcroft Road but was renamed May Street in July 1887.

11

Queen Mary's School

The origins of the school we now know as Queen Mary's are found in a medieval religious guild, "the gild of the Holy Ghost" or "the brotherhood of the Chapel of the Holy Ghost". It is not certain when this guild was founded, but it was certainly in existence early in the thirteenth century, for in 1214, with the lifting of the Papal Interdict of 1208, which had forbidden the people of the town to bury their dead in the parish graveyard, a chapel was built to the north of the town. A priest was appointed to take the services in this chapel and also to act as chaplain to the Guild.

Although in the beginning the priest seems to have had no educational duties to perform, in course of time these seem to have been undertaken. In 1524, Lord Sandys of the Vyne obtained from Henry VIII a charter which gave the Guild the right to hold property. It appears from a chantry certificate of 1548 that from its legal incorporation in November, 1524, some of the Guild's money was employed "to fynde a scole master to teche children grammar". The sum of £5 17s. 8d. a year was paid to the schoolmaster for his services.

The Guild, which escaped suppression under Henry VIII, did however suffer this fate under Edward VI, when its properties were sold for £1,675. This did not result in the interruption of the educational work of the Guild, for it was supported by Crown revenues during the whole of Edward VI's reign. It is on record that payment of £5 17s. 8d. a year was paid to Thomas Browne, "schoolmaster of the grammar school, founded by a certain gild called the Fraternities in Basingstoke". Thomas Browne was Vicar of Basingstoke.

Mary Tudor came to the throne in 1553, and in the following year, in response to a petition from the townspeople, she re-founded the Guild by the granting of a new charter. This restored to the Guild the right to own lands and derive income from them. The charter specifically stated that a priest should be appointed to conduct the services in the Chapel "and for the instruction of the youths and boys of the said town".

The affairs of the Guild for the next hundred years are recorded in the Wardens' accounts (for the period from 1557 to 1654). These show among other things that the corporation of the town gradually assumed control of the Guild, through the administration of its estates. By 1654, the officers of the Guild were also members of the Corporation; there were nearly one hundred members and the Vicar of Basingstoke was the chief of these.

What of the school itself—the actual building? This was a half-timbered building consisting of one large room situated on the foundations of the western tower of the original chapel. It appears to have been demolished in 1636, and then rebuilt by a man called Edwards who was paid £11 for the work. Repairs were carried out to the school in 1652–3; presumably these were necessary because of damage and neglect during the Cromwellian period. Both the Guild and the school seem to have been suppressed during this time.

The story of the Guild and the school from 1639 onwards is a somewhat confused one, mainly because of the disputes which arose between the various masters of the school and the Corporation. One of these disputes involved Edward Webbe; Webbe had been appointed by letters patent of Charles I to be minister and schoolmaster for life. This appointment entitled him to the revenues from the Guild lands, in return for conducting services in the Chapel and teaching in the school. A sequestration order was made against Webbe, which deprived him of the emoluments to which he was entitled. These passed to the Corporation, while his position as master seems to have been filled by one Pocock during the period 1649–55. In 1667, Webbe renewed his claim to his position and emoluments. Eventually both he and the Corporation agreed to submit this dispute to an arbitrator, Bishop Morley. In 1669 the Bishop decided against Webbe but out of the arbitration came a decision that the Bishop should appoint the master, who, during his term of office would be entitled to all rents and profits of the estate. The decision did not, however, put an end to the argument, for on at least two occasions during the eighteenth century (in 1717 and 1744) there were further petitionings against the Corporation. The second of these was made by the Rev. S. Loggon, who wrote a history of the Guild in support of his claim. Both petitions were unsuccessful.

In 1825 Parliament appointed commissioners to review the functioning of charitable bodies, including those engaged in education. The report on Queen Mary's School shows that there was a master appointed by the Crown and an usher appointed by the Corporation. The master at the time of the report was the Rev. William Workman and his income was £150. The average number of pupils was stated to be 12 and they were all fee-paying, boys from the town paid 15s. a quarter, and those from the surrounding country £1 a quarter. The subjects studied were classics, history, geography, writing and arithmetic. The master considered himself bound only to teach classics.

In 1852 the School underwent a re-organisation; eight trustees were appointed; the headmaster was to be appointed by the Crown but his appointment was subject to approval by the Bishop.

On 29th May, 1855, the foundation stone of the "new" Queen Mary's School was laid in Worting Road, then very much still open country. The Mayor performed the ceremony "with much pomp and ceremony, ringing of bells, music playing, dinner parties, etc.".

Eighty-five years later, in the summer of 1940, the School was transferred to larger premises at Vyne Road, and for the first time in its history the Headmaster was not a Clerk in Holy Orders.

XXIII Queen Anne House, Church Street, in 1964

XXIV Winchester Street and Winton Square, about 1910

XXV The Market Place, about 1928, with two cafés within yards of each other

XXVI Basingstoke Town Hall, with Clock Tower, about 1910

XXVII Eastern Basingstoke: taken from the Town Hall Clock Tower in 1960, this shows the Central Car Park, New Road, Eastrop and the countryside beyond

XXVIII The area of Town Centre demolition, taken from the old Town Hall Clock Tower, prior to 1961

XXIX The Black Dam, before it was reduced in size to make a roundabout to give access to the M3 Motorway

XXX A scene of desolation, after partial demolition of Potters Lane, in 1966

12

Old Inns

(Reproduced by kind permission of the *Hants & Berks Gazette,* who published this essay in January, 1932.)

For untold generations the inn has been one of the essential factors of an established community. Wherever settled conditions allowed of peaceable travel, some place of rest and refreshment became necessary. Even the African kraal has its empty hut for the traveller and while its connection through the wayside tavern to the "Grand Babylon Hotel" seems remote, it is none the less actual and natural. In the medieval times of our own land the inn with its tradition of good food, abundant hospitality and sociable atmosphere, played a much more important part in public life than it does today. Dr. Johnson described the occupancy of a tavern chair as the height of felicity, and to a man of his expansive temperament the convivial atmosphere of the inn must have given him the exact environment he enjoyed. In the smaller towns and villages, where news depended on the verbal report of actual travellers, the advent of a stranger would naturally concern the local gossips, and the spontaneous adjournment to the inn—to see and hear the "latest"—tended to make it a social centre for the surrounding inhabitants.

The changing conditions and tastes of the last hundred years have served rather to emphasise the social character of the inn, with its provision of refreshment, usually liquid and alcoholic. However much we may deprecate certain aspects of its expression, the social and friendly spirit of the inn at its best has for centuries formed an essential element in national life.

That the inn served some useful purpose seems indicated by its frequency, especially in a small market town like Basingstoke. Market Day, a hundred years ago, drawing to the town the agricultural community for miles around, must have made exceptional demands on available accommodation, from the larger hostelries where the wealthier farmers congregated to the humbler beer-house that catered for the carter and drover. Even so, at first sight, 75 inns in the borough with a town population of about 3,600 seems a fairly adequate provision. Yet some such number appears in a detailed list of the inns of 1836 left by the late Mr. W. Hall of Church Street, as related to him by his father, the late Mr. John Hall.

At that time much of the original business of the inn would still be in dealing with the relatively large road transport that preceded the railway, but which in later years dwindled to a merely local traffic, until resuscitated by the motor car. Pigot's Directory of about this date gives the following coaches as calling at the local inns every day: to London, 17;

to Southampton, 6; Devonport, 5; Exeter and Salisbury, 2 each; Taunton and Weymouth, 1 each; with 2 to Reading and 1 to Bridgwater three times a week. There was also a service of waggons and carts for the conveyance of goods, but these were advertised as starting from the Wharf, Flaxpool and Staple Hall (where was this?). Also Crowley's and Birnie's barges and fly boats left for London by canal three times a week.

Besides these semi-official services there must have been innumerable private vehicles on the road, which had to put up for the night at some convenient public house. Hence it is not so anomalous as at first appears that inns should be grouped in rows of three or four at certain strategical street corners. At the top of Oat (Wote) Street would be seen The Feathers, next door The Fox and Hounds (now Willis'), two doors farther on another inn of unknown name (now Thelenberg's); across the Market Place on the London Street side The George, with The Fleur-de-Lys (now Boyer's) close by, and The Bell (now Lipton's) opposite; while on the Church Street side would be The Royal Oak (where the Town Hall now stands), with The Ship (now Ford's) a few yards farther on, while down the street stood The Black Boy and beyond this The Eagle (now forming part of Messrs. G. Stevens, Ltd).

Again at the top of Flaxpool, now called Flaxfield, would be found The Star (now Long Lodge), The Pear Tree, a private brewery with an actual pear tree in front, The Green Dragon (now the lodging house) and The Pheasant a few doors beyond it.

Bunnian Place appears to have been an important channel of traffic to judge from the facilities it offered in the threefold group of Queen's Arms, Jolly Farmer and Royal Oak at the top; The Prince of Wales (lately Viney's forge), The House at Home and the Old House at Home at the bottom; while The Olive Branch stood behind The Castle at the end of the passage from Bunnian Place to Reading Road.

Chapel Street, as one of the oldest streets in the town, had its Rising Sun and Half Moon at the top of the hill; its Crown and Cushion (previously The Black Cow) half way down; with The Rose and Crown at the bottom but the site of a much earlier inn of about 1600 (The Holy Lamb in the White Waye) has not yet been ascertained, although it may be included in the old half-timbered houses still standing.

The Flower Pots (later Hackwood nurseries), The Black Horse (facing Brambly's Lane), and The Rose (supposed to have been replaced by the Friends' Meeting House) have all disappeared, while The Skipper's Inn has developed into the attractive private residence Skippett's House.

It appears possible that The Red Lion, in its last reconstruction may have absorbed one if not more earlier places of refreshment. Mr. Hall's list makes reference to a porter shop apparently on or near the site of The Red Lion, while there is a record of 1755 describing a somewhat imposing hostelry: "A mansion house, a gate room and a passage under the gate-house chamber—formerly The Three Mariners, on the north side of London Street." It seemed feasible that The Anchor might have been the lineal descendant of The Three Mariners. Unfortunately for this theory however, the name of The Anchor in 1762 was The Chequers.

It has become so customary to name public houses by their sign that the curious fact may be overlooked that it is the inn almost alone that has retained the once universal method of announcing its business by picture rather than print. In medieval times every tradesman advertised his shop by an appropriate sign to such an extent that in big cities passers-by were gravely inconvenienced. After the Fire of London, which cleared away many of these obstructions, the custom gradually died out with the exception—until recently—of the barber's or barber-surgeon's pole, the golden balls of the pawnbroker and the inn signboard. It is of interest to note that even in Roman times the tavern made its appeal to the public by the universally recognised sign of a bush of evergreen suspended from a pole, whence arose the dictum: "good wine needs no bush". With the general use of signs, the inn extended its choice of symbol in many directions. An old retainer might provide accommodation for overflow guests at the Castle and hang up a copy of his lord's escutcheon as an indication of the fact, and the innkeeper might be occupied in some form of industry and so associate the insignia of his craft with his "house". The range of material seems endless, as there are reputed to be over 2,000 differing signs in Hampshire alone. They can be loosely classified into categories such as national or loyal, ecclesiastical, heraldic, industrial, sporting, etc., although each division tends to merge into the rest.

In the first category, there are, or were, locally:

The Queen's Head (somewhere "near the market") usually ascribed to Queen Elizabeth, but probably adjusted to later political conditions.

The King's Arms (site unknown) and The Queen's Arms (afterwards The Fox and Hounds, now Willis') which may refer to the edicts of James I and Charles II that their escutcheons should be exhibited in churches and public buildings as an inducement to loyalty.

The Prince of Wales, and The Royal Oak commemorating the escape of Charles II with the more general emblems of The Rose (the Tudor badge), The Crown, The Crown and Cushion, and The Rose and Crown.

The George is usually connected with the patron saint of that name, rather than with royalty—St. George was in high repute about 1415—about the period of Agincourt—and several Hampshire inns at Alresford and Winchester were renamed in his honour, among which may be our local example,

The Self Defence (formerly Defence not Defiance) suggests the date of 1803, when Volunteer Corps were raised all over the country, including Basingstoke, in reply to Napoleon's threat of invasion.

The Olive Branch apparently commemorates a celebration of peace, and The Soldier's Return its fitting and happy sequel, while The Royal Exchange may have some association of a national character.

Among ecclesiastical emblems we find, first and foremost The Angel (now Barclays Bank), perhaps the most famous of local hostelries, whence issued not inappropriately the fund "for repairing the Causey to the Church".

The Anchor, from its association elsewhere with Hope to be regarded as a religious symbol and The Cross Keys (now The Angel) were the arms of several English Bishoprics.

The heraldic group yield quite naturally the abnormally tinted animals:

The Golden Lion, The White Lion (probably G. H. Webber's), and The Red Lion from the or, argent and gules of the Herald's Office.

The White Hart, while possibly a sporting emblem was, when gold-collared as at Worting, the badge of Richard II. The Feathers convey a reminder of The Black Prince, while The Rising Sun was the badge of the Percy's. The Green Dragon represents the evil influence of the parish as opposed to its Patron Saint, and on the Feast of Rogation was carried in procession to be severely maltreated at the conclusion of the ceremonies.

Clearly in the sporting group were The Fox (somewhere in Flaxfield), The Fox and Hounds, The Hare and Hounds, The Stag and Hounds, The Black Horse, and The Horse and Jockey, the latter being evidently connected with the races on Basingstoke Down. Among the familiar objects of a country town are The Lamb, The Goat, The Swan, The Pheasant, The Black Cow (afterwards The Crown and Cushion), The Eagle (probably heraldic rather than local), and The Falcon (now Boyer's) which may have had a hawking association or represent the noble family of the Dukes of Bolton, whose crest it was.

The industrial section gives The Three Tuns (now Darracott's), the arms of the Vintners Company, suggesting like The Grapes, the manufacturer of wine; The Brown Jug (somewhere in Worting) a homely and appropriate sign of the trade, The Plough, The Harrow, The Waggon and Horses, The Ship (probably The Sheep), all recently vanished. Others were The Wheatsheaf, The Cattle Market with The Jolly Farmer (once at the top of Bunnian Place) as a fitting climax, and The Barge, reminiscent of the time when water played a large part in inland transport. Skipper's Inn, on the Harrow Way, doubtless offered special inducements of secrecy and protection to seafaring travellers along the old Pack Lane, engaged among other things in evading the Excise officers. The Pear Tree probably took its name from an actual pear tree, while The Bell and The Flower Pots seem to have little association with anything but these specific articles.

The Four Horse Shoes, while natural to a farming district, may contain the farrier's arms of three horse shoes, with one more added for luck! The Traveller's Rest and The House at Home appropriately convey the ideal of an inn, but The Railway Arms and The Engineer's Arms have little meaning beyond a reference to their frequenters. The Bolton Arms (formerly The Maidenhead, now Ody's) does relate, as so may inns do, to the local landed family. It is not easy to explain its previous name, The Maidenhead, although suggestions have been offered that it may indicate the Blessed Virgin or Queen Elizabeth. The Trial, which preceded The Junction is also a puzzling problem in derivation. The Black Boy, representing a diminutive negro from the plantations, usually indicates the sale of tobacco as well as the customary liquid commodities, while The Shades (now the Victoria Brewery) is a sign frequently associated with a small bar or tap attached to a brewery or large hotel.

It is probable that other onetime inns must have entirely disappeared and their memory has been lost. Who can now say where The Queen's Head was?—unless it be the "old inn" (now Thelenberg's). Similarly no one seems to know the exact site of The Brown Jug at Worting, or The

Fox at Flaxfield. It is now doubtful if we shall ever prove that The Gridiron preceded Angel's shop.

The most likely source of information, reliable on this and many other phases of bygone social life is to be found in the title deeds of local properties. Old parchments and documents have an enormous value for the student of history. The new Law of Property has rendered many of them obsolete and of no legal value, but their destruction is none the less a crime against the best interests of the State.

(*Editor's Note*: At the time of writing this essay, Messrs. Willis and Ellaway added a tabulated list of these old inns, together with a sketch map of their respective locations, in the Willis Museum. With it they included a sketch map showing distribution of inns of Basingstoke in 1932. It was interesting in the 1930s to note that there were approximately half the number of inns there had been in the 1830s.)

13

The Twentieth Century: preparation for the New Town

In 1930, when the population of the town was about 14,000, a Mr. C. C. Clark, speaking to the Rotary Club of Basingstoke on the theme: "The architectural development of Basingstoke" gave a description of the site and important features of the town before going on to make suggestions for its future development. He mentioned "the market place with its curious clock-tower" and continued: "traffic immediately confronts us, traffic of every description from enormous stacks of milk churns on wheels to the normal small car. Obviously the road is too small for the traffic".

Mr. Clark was the first to express publicly the view that Basingstoke's future was bound up with the extension of industry, making the point that good transport facilities were essential.

Basingstoke has always possessed the asset of natural nodality: the meeting of important routes at or near the town. Before the coming of the railway, the main means of communication between different parts of the country was the stage coach. Basingstoke served as a convenient staging-post on the great coachway road which linked London with the south and west. Fifty coaches a day are said to have called here at one time, thirty a week was usual for many years. Basingstoke was also linked to London by the Basingstoke to River Wey Canal in 1796, but this neither carried the tonnage expected nor earned the revenue necessary to make it a commercial enterprise. It did, however, help to make Basingstoke more of a distributing centre, for example goods were consigned to Basingstoke for onward transport by means of horse drawn wagon to Southampton and Salisbury. This role it fulfilled only while an easy movement along the Channel was restricted during the wars with France and until the canal's doom was sealed by the coming of the railway.

An alternative view on the expansion of the town was put forward in 1937. Mr. P. M. Crosse, a traffic consultant, spoke in the town of the advantages of electrifying the railway between Basingstoke and London. After referring to building development taking place in and around the town, he said "the prosperity of Basingstoke tradespeople would take an upward turn with increased residential population". Both Mr. Clark and Mr. Crosse were in favour of controlled development of the town, but whereas one favoured the growth of employment in the town, the other thought more in terms of the town becoming a dormitory for London.

It would be wrong to think that the town itself neglected consideration of growth. Early in 1930 the proposal was put forward (under the Local Government Act, 1929) for the extension of the boundaries of the borough to include Basing, Cliddesden and Worting. The Rural District Council asked for assurances (which were not forthcoming) that the Borough of Basingstoke would guarantee the provision of sewerage, water and electricity services within ten years of a possible incorporation. Much discussion went on in Basing regarding the possible incorporation, but the majority of the inhabitants were opposed to the plan.

. . . . . .

Towards the end of 1931, the Finance Committee of the Borough Council reported that it had considered a letter received from the Basingstoke Chamber of Commerce, which asked the Council to form a Development Committee. It was agreed that a conference should be called to discuss ways in which new industries might be attracted to the town. As a direct result of this, the Basingstoke Development Committee was set up; it consisted of representatives of the Borough Council, the Chamber of Commerce, the Trades Council and the Rotary Club. Eventually a booklet was produced called "Basingstoke for Industry". This listed the available sites, names of owners and acreage. In the booklet, the town was stated as having "many special features as a provincial industrial town on account of its geographical position". Reference was made to its suitability in respect of transport facilities and also to the availability of labour, both within the Borough and from the neighbouring villages. Initially little resulted from the efforts of the Development Committee to attract new industry to the town. It did report though in 1933, that it had received some enquiries, including two from Switzerland and one from Italy, the latter being for a factory to employ 300.

Meanwhile the town continued to depend largely on the prosperity of the two important engineering firms (Wallis and Steevens, and Thorneycrofts, the two clothing firms (Gerrish, Ames and Simpkins, and Mares) and on market gardening carried on at the Cranbourne Lane Nurseries. The farming of the surrounding region also continued to exercise an important influence on the economy of the town, in its function as a market and shopping centre.

Basingstoke was not unaffected by the depression of the 30's, but unemployment was not as serious here as in the heavy industrial areas of the north and South Wales.

This was a period when newer industries were tending to locate themselves nearer their chief markets, taking advantage of greater mobility resulting from the increased use of electricity as a source of power and of the motor vehicle as a means of transport. One result of this trend was the growth of the concentrations of London and Birmingham, whose problems (and the allied decline of some of the older industrial areas) were investigated by the Barlow Commission which began its work in 1937. Among other measures, the Commission recommended the dispersal of industry and the industrial population from the congested urban areas of the country.

The Greater London Plan of 1944 (the Abercrombie Plan) took note of these recommendations and proposed the dispersal of over one million people from the metropolitan area. Together with Aylesbury and Bletchley, Basingstoke was included in the category "additions to existing towns outside the Greater London Plan boundaries, mostly between forty and fifty miles from the centre of London". Of Basingstoke's suitability for expansion the Plan said: "This is a railway junction and is also on the Exeter Road. It is a thriving market and shopping centre serving a wide district. Of recent years, the town has tended to expand industrially and is well located for the reception of certain types of industry, including also engineering, food factories, and other concerns needing a clean atmosphere". It was proposed that Basingstoke should receive 20,000 people from the Greater London Plan area.

The industrial expansion referred to was caused mainly by the arrival of two new firms in the town; in 1937 a new factory for the manufacture of aircraft instruments was opened by the Glasgow firm of Kelvin, Bottomley and Baird, and in 1939 the American firm of Eli Lilly started the manufacture of pharmaceutical products.

. . . . .

In March 1945, the Planning Officer for the Basingstoke area spoke on the future of the town; he referred to possible changes making the point that these would depend "on the ultimate size of the town and whether it might be required to take some overspill from London". Two years later the Borough Council received a report from its Finance Committee about the Greater London Plan to include Basingstoke among towns to be expanded. The report drew attention to the need to ensure a careful selection of the type of industry, so that there would be suitable diversity of employment in the town. It also mentioned the need for a building programme which would ensure that houses and factories would be erected concurrently and for an appropriate expansion of the various service industries.

The Hampshire County Council referred to the expansion proposals for the town at its meeting in November 1947 and asked that it should be given an opportunity of joining with the Borough Council in any discussions which might take place. Further discussions of the proposals to expand the town took place at a meeting of the North-East Hampshire Planning Committee held early in January 1950. At this gathering, the Area Planning Officer spoke about plans to enlarge the town's population to about 35,000. The Committee Chairman, Alderman Mussellwhite said that the Borough Council were, generally speaking in favour of the proposal, thinking it logical for the town to grow. There was however some fear that the town might grow too large. The Town Clerk emphasised that Basingstoke would not become a "new town", but would merely undergo accelerated expansion. He added that the Borough Council had acquired 90 acres of land off the Kingsclere Road (the Houndmills area) to provide accommodation for factories and housing for the decentralised population.

By the provisions of the Town and Country Planning Act, 1947 each County Council was required to make a survey of the resources in its area and to publish a report and a plan for the future use of land within its boundaries. The Hampshire Development Plan 1950 contained proposals for the accommodation within Basingstoke of the overspill population envisaged by the Greater London Plan. Assuming that this would be the 20,000 proposed and that there would be a natural increase of 3,230 over a period of 20 years it would put the 1971 population figure at 40,000. Of this number, one half would constitute the total working population, of which it was estimated 10,000 would be employed in secondary or manufacturing industry. To accommodate this industry it was recognised that more land would have to be made available, and the Plan proposed to increase the industrial acreage within Basingstoke from 80 to 225 acres by 1971. The main areas set aside for secondary industry, in addition to the Thorneycroft and Brook Street areas were to be the northern or Kingsclere Road area and the southern or Winchester Road area. For both of these areas light industrial projects were proposed. Long term proposals included the transfer of industry from Station Hill and Worting to the new industrial areas of the town.

The original proposed development plan was later modified to take account of the need to preserve land of high agricultural value in the immediate neighbourhood of the town. The main modification was the reduction of the size of the immigrant population and thus a revision of the target population for 1971 from 40,000 to 32,000. A new development plan drawn up in 1955 repeated this new estimate of population increase; it also allocated a further five acres of land for industrial purposes.

Meanwhile the Town Development Act 1952 had been passed. This made it possible for local authorities of small towns some distance from large and congested urban areas to receive financial assistance towards expansion and development where required. In December 1952 the Area Planning Officer reported that the London County Council had made tentative approaches about accommodating overspill population in the town. An initial building programme of 1,500 houses was envisaged.

. . . . .

1955 was the year when the future of the town suddenly seemed to become the concern of everyone; until then it was mostly the official bodies who had discussed the expansion scheme, but from 1955 the man in the street began to take active interest.

It was to be expected that there would be different views on the rightness or otherwise of the proposals. One view was expressed at the NFU dinner held in February. The deputy Mayor, Mr. Stroud, stated it to be his opinion that the LCC scheme was not for the betterment of the town in the long run. He thought that too many council houses were being built and that rate-producing private housing should be increased to counterbalance the cost of providing council houses and as a means of releasing the council houses for those who really needed them. He mentioned a scheme whereby private enterprise would build 500 houses and also factories.

Another view on the proposal to expand the town was expressed in a prepared statement by Mr. Howard who reported that a delegation would be meeting the LCC; this would not in any way commit the Borough Council, it was to be purely exploratory. Alderman Mussellwhite said he was glad that the statement had been made and that the Borough was still uncommitted at that stage. No-one was in a position to give a considered opinion on the desirability or otherwise of the plan but natural growth alone would involve an expansion of the services of the town; there would need to be an expansion of the water and sewerage systems and changes would have to be made in the centre of the town. This would be necessary, LCC scheme or no; he suggested that the cost of providing these could in fact be less if the LCC scheme were adopted.

Mr. Stroud reiterated strong opposition to the proposal saying that it was not in the interests of the citizens of the Borough. Mr. Weston agreed and added his worry of the possible loss of good farming land; he stressed that the Borough should concern itself with housing its own people first.

The correspondence column of the local newspaper began to print letters received regarding the proposed expansion. One of the earliest of these came from a local firm of estate agents, who advocated, perhaps not surprisingly, the use of private money for the building of houses, shops, factories and offices. The houses built could be leased in block leases to the council and the factories, offices and shops could be for sale or rental; this would have the advantage of giving the town control of its own development, thus there would be little or no burden on the rates.

The County Council anyway, as Planning Authority, would have to play a major part in deciding on the implementation of any proposal. In March 1955 at a meeting of the Hampshire County Council, Mr. L. J. Smart asked for sympathetic consideration by the Council of the proposal to expand the town. The occasion was the report to the Council of its Finance Committee. This report said that the County Planning Committee had been asked in May 1953 to consider the town's expansion and since then discussions had gone on between officials of the three authorities. After saying that a vociferous and powerful opposition to the LCC scheme had grown up, Mr. Smart gave it as his opinion that it was in the interests of Basingstoke to bring to early fruition negotiations with the LCC. The Chairman of the County Council said that it was for Basingstoke itself to decide.

There was no doubt that there was concern about the likely financial burden on the rate-payers of the town. It was thought (and indeed publicly stated by some) that the LCC was trying to solve its housing problems on the cheap and that it should be prepared to contribute in such a way that there would be "no charge on the rates now or in the future". It was not known at this stage what the LCC was willing to do, nor had anyone any idea to what extent the Government would assist financially with the scheme.

On 10th February, a delegation from the Borough Council met representatives of the County Council and with them members of the LCC. This meeting resolved that a joint approach be made to the Minister of Housing and Local Government, in order to find out his reaction to the proposal and especially to ascertain what financial assistance would be available.

On 26th April, the Borough Council received a letter from the Minister which gave the information that half the cost of new water and sewerage works in towns undergoing expansion would be met by a government grant provided that the places were suitable and that the scale and rate of the expansion were moderate. Details were also given of the method of sharing the liability for statutory rate contribution between the exporting and receiving authorities. The exporting authority would be responsible for statutory rate contribution for ten years or such longer period as agreed by the two authorities. If after ten years the rate burden on the receiving authority was too great, there would be an Exchequer grant to meet all or part of this burden as appropriate.

It was then possible for the town to undergo a deliberate planned expansion over a definite number of years with financial assistance from the central government. The alternative to this would be expansion by private development, with no financial assistance for water and sewerage works and perhaps without the provision of employment in the growing town.

It is appropriate here to set these local developments against the background of those taking place elsewhere. In a progress report made to the LCC on 25th October, 1955 by its Housing and Town Planning Committees it was stated that there was an increasing need for the Council to look outside its boundaries, if it was to be able to conform to its Development Plan as approved by the Minister. Already of course, much dispersal of employment and people had taken place to the new towns. In addition, limited overspill agreements had been made with Swindon, Bletchley and Daventry under the 1952 Town Development Act. Some implementation of these agreements had already taken place in Bletchley and Swindon. Initially the Minister had agreed in principle to allow negotiations with only a limited number of other towns; of these priority was to be given to Ashford (Kent), Basingstoke, Letchworth and Peterborough. Later, in June 1955 he had said that there was no objection to negotiations with Bury St. Edmunds, Thetford, Haverhill and Huntingdon. Following further representations, the LCC was able to negotiate with towns over a wide area south-east of a line from the Wash to the Solent. The report went on to say that negotiations were in fact in progress with the following towns in addition to those mentioned above: Aylesbury, Grantham, Kettering, Luton and Dunstable, and Wellingborough, even though three of these were outside "the Wash to the Solent" line.

Two other interesting points were mentioned in the report: it was stated that the County Councils had been asked to suggest which towns within their boundaries were suitable for expansion, and that a conference of their representatives was to be held at County Hall on 18th November; perhaps even more interesting (in view of the scheme that was later put forward for a new town at Hook) was the proposal that the Minister be asked to create a new town under the 1946 New Towns Act. It was suggested that the LCC should have strong representation on the Development Corporation which would be set up to develop this town.

The LCC had in fact been investigating the possibilities of building a new town somewhere in the region permitted by the Minister of Housing and Local Government. In all some 70 sites for a new town within 50 miles of London were looked at. One of the sites investigated was Hook, and the idea of a new town assumed a more definite form with publication in

October 1958 of a proposal to develop the area around Hook as a town for "upwards of 100,000 people". The proposal met with opposition from many quarters. For example Hartley Wintney RDC opposed the scheme on the grounds that it would destroy the rural character of the area and result in the loss of good agricultural land. The publication of the Hook plan seems to have aroused some doubts about the intentions of the LCC in respect of expansion proposals for Basingstoke. The opinion was even expressed that the LCC did not appear to be so keen to reach an agreement with the Basingstoke Borough Council.

The meeting of the Hampshire County Council on 25th November, 1958, discussed the Hook scheme; no member spoke in favour of it, many in fact were strongly opposed to it, some on the grounds that they did not wish to see the county industrialised and thought the overspill should be directed elsewhere. This argument was coupled with the argument about the necessity of possessing agricultural land. The attitude of the members of the Council can perhaps be attributed to a concern about adding to the problems the county was already having to face; already rapid growth of population by immigration independent of any overspill proposals was obvious throughout the county, adding to which the growth of population in the three county boroughs (Portsmouth, Southampton and Bournemouth) were giving rise to small scale overspill problems. There was also the fear of too great a concentration of urban development in an area already very urbanised: Hook would be in the centre of a group of growing towns—Aldershot, Farnborough, Fleet, Camberley, Wokingham, Reading and of course, Basingstoke.

Although there was some expression of dislike of the way in which the LCC had gone about the Hook scheme, there was also a feeling that it would be a mistake to refuse pointblank to have anything to do with their proposals. In fact, the view eventually prevailed that the correct procedure was to look at the question of overspill in a wider context than had been done. The council should hear a good deal more of the LCC's case and approach discussions with an open mind.

Eventually these discussions took place between the Hampshire County Council and the LCC covering the whole field of overspill policy so far as it might affect Hampshire. These discussions produced an alternative scheme, whereby overspill population from London would be accommodated by the expansion of Andover, Basingstoke and Tadley.

This alternative proposal was adopted by the LCC on 11th November, 1960, and on 31st October, 1961, a tripartite agreement was signed, under the terms of which Basingstoke was to expand over a period of 15 years to become a town with a population of over 80,000. The actual agreement between the three authorities was for the erection of 11,500 dwellings. This major scheme replaced the smaller one (agreed to in October 1959) which involved the building of 3,500 houses for an overspill population of about 11,000 to 12,000.

. . . . . .

Since then Basingstoke has changed radically; first of all the new bus station replaced the old terminus by the Barge Inn; then the New Market

Square was built close by. Demolition of the lower part of Wote Street and Potters Lane then began in earnest, in their place the raised shopping precinct and the multi-storey car park (soon to be one of the largest in Europe) began to be built.

Thus in building the new Basingstoke, many of the streets, lanes, shops, inns and houses mentioned in this book no longer exist. But they remain in our memories and the town's archives for ever.

Appendices

(i) *MAIDENWELL*

(Reproduced by kind permission of the *Hants & Berks Gazette*)

High up on the wolds of Lincolnshire, but sheltered in a shallow fold of the downs, stands a spacious and handsome farmhouse, on the front of which a Basingstoke visitor may well be surprised to find a foundation stone bearing the names of the Mayor, Aldermen and Councillors of Basingstoke, while high over the porch, carved in stone, are the Borough Arms, similar to those on the Town Hall and Corn Exchange. This farmhouse, with its extensive farm buildings and its 1,400 acres of farmland around them form the Maidenwell Estate, which, with other detached fields and woods in Lincolnshire have been for 200 years a very valuable asset to the Corporation of Basingstoke. To trace the association of this property 180 miles away to our town we have to turn back to the days of Queen Elizabeth, and in particular to one of her distinguished seamen, who not only left cause for grateful remembrance to his native town but left the imprint of his name on the American continent and made a definite contribution to the establishment of the British Empire in India.

Sir James Lancaster was born in Basingstoke where, it is stated, he was greatly helped in his younger years by the benefactions of the Corporation, a fact that he appears to have gratefully remembered throughout a very eventful life. He appears at first to have combined the offices of soldier and merchant. From 1591 to 1595 he was engaged in expeditions to the East Indies, but in 1599 he was appointed General of the Fleet of the newly formed East India Company, sailing for India in 1600, whence he returned three years later, being knighted on his return from a successful voyage. He was interested also in voyages of exploration at a time when Europe was discovering and appropriating the rest of the world and it is due to his activities in the promotion of expeditions to find the Northwest Passage that Lancaster Sound still bears this Basingstoke man's name . . .

He evidently became a man of considerable means for in 1618 he was the owner of extensive properties in Lincolnshire and in Pamber, Hampshire . . .

In his Will dated 18th April, 1618, he directed that his Trustees should hand over to the Skinners' Company, the income derived from the trust, charging the Company with the payment therefrom of the following charitable bequests for ever, a total sum of £103 6s. 8d. to Basingstoke, made up as follows: £30 "for such poor people who are of honest report and who frequent to hear the weekly lecture"; £40 to be added to his cousin Sir James Deane's previous bequest of £10 towards the maintenance of an honest, sufficient and learned preacher as lecturer; £20 (£16 to the usher and £4 to the master of the Free School) if the schoolmaster was approved by the bailiffs, otherwise the Company to spend it at their discretion; £13 6s. 8d. towards the maintenance of a petty schoolmaster "to teach little children to write and read, and especially to read and learn the Catechism of the principles of religion".

There were also charges for the benefit of Kingsclere which seems to have shared the affection of Sir James . . .

About 1712 difficulties began to arise about the payment of the various charities, the Skinners' Company finding the income from the trust properties insufficient, as they said, to meet the charges. For some time they seem to have made partial payments, in some cases half their liabilities. So the disappointed recipients, Basingstoke Corporation, brought charges against the Company in 1712 and again the following year. Later the Corporation put forward a proposal that in order to relieve the situation, the property of the trust should be transferred to them, together with its liabilities, they giving security to pay all the charges levied on the estate of Sir James Lancaster and to keep a public register of their management of the funds. The Company fought this plan, but the Lord Chancellor "declared that the said trust ought to be transferred to the Mayor, Aldermen and Burgesses of Basingstoke and doth order and decree the same accordingly". Having regard to the fact that the charities payable—and still paid—from the Lancaster estate total £251 13s. 4d. and the income therefrom must often have exceeded £2,000 per annum, it would appear that Basingstoke made a very good bargain.

In the year 1854 the Corporation were receiving a net total of £1,263 from the Lancaster bequest; in 1873 it had risen to £2,155; in 1879 up to £2,757. The total Lancaster Charities paid, then and now, amount to £251, so that even now when the depression in the agricultural world has severely reduced the income from these estates, they still remain a source of great financial help to the ratepayers of Basingstoke, a fact that shoud serve to keep the name of Sir James Lancaster in their grateful remembrance.

(ii) *PRIMITIVE SUN DIALS (OR SCRATCH DIALS)*

(Reproduced by kind permission of the *Hants & Berks Gazette*)

Incised upon the walls of our parish churches are often to be found a series of patterns consisting, in their most elementary form, a number of lines radiating downwards from a hole which may be either in the face of a stone or in a joint of the masonry. A casual inspection would probably pronounce them as sundials, and some are undoubtedly so. But the actual designs are extremely varied, and many appear to be relatively useless—and deliberately so—for timekeeping purposes. The correlation and comparison of a large number of these dials has revealed certain definite tendencies in the position and relative importance of certain of these radiating lines, and the conclusion has been reached that in these dials a primitive method of ascertaining not the hour of the day but of services, hence the alternative name of "service dial". The parish priest in the pre-Reformation era appears to have adopted the use of this simple expedient to indicate the hour of his regular services, especially that of the celebration of the Mass at 9 a.m. which hour is frequently emphasised on the dial . . .

In the Basingstoke district a survey was made in 1917 of upward of 60 parish churches. Of these about 12 were deducted as being new buildings or plaster covered; from the remaining 48 or 50, 12 were found to bear dials varying in number from one to eight as detailed below:

ASHE. Dial, at the lower left corner of centre window on north side of the nave. Stylehole in stone. Traces of circle 5½ in diameter. Vertical line distinct, other lines apparently dividing semi-circle into ten equal parts, very faint and indistinct. Its position on the north side of the church indicates removal of window masonry from the south.

BAUGHURST. Two dials both inverted. On the west doorway: (1) on the lowest stone course on right side. Stylehole in stone with three concentric circles of 2 in, 3 in, and 4 in diameters with three radial lines extending to outer circle; one vertical above stylehole and one on either side at an angle of 45° to vertical. (2) Second stone course left side. Stylehole in mortar joint. Five radiating lines about 5 in long; one vertical, one on either side at 45° to vertical, and a scratched line on either side at 10° to 15° to vertical, the vertical and two right lines ending in small holes; the 9 o'clock line clearly cut.

BRAMLEY. Three dials with several small copy dials, on south doorway of chancel. (1) Left side of door, 3 ft 6 in above ground level. Stylehole in stone, full circle, 7 in diameter. Lines so weathered as to be indefinite; later scratches added. The whole partly cemented over. (2) On right side of door about 5 ft above ground. Stylehole in stone, full circle, 6 in diameter. Lower semicircle divided into 12 equal parts, but two lines on right weathered out. All radii end in holes on the circle. (3) 2 ft below (2). Stylehole in stone, irregular and obviously damaged; full circle, 6 in diameter. No horizontal line, vertical line original with six or seven other lines. Some probably original, but defaced by later scratchings. Two small copy dials on doorway with one on the wall inside doorway.

HERRIARD. Eight dials, one on south doorway and seven on southeast buttress of nave. (1) On right of door, about 2 ft 6 in above ground; inverted stylehole in mortar joint forming horizontal line. Five lines about 4 in long, the three on the right ending in holes, the other two probably being later scratches. (2) Face of south-east buttress of nave. Fourth stone course above ground level, left side. Stylehole in stone, no circle or lines. Three holes 4–5 in from stylehole in lower left quadrant. (3) Fourth course right side. Stylehole in stone, ½ in wide, 1 in deep. No circle or horizontal line. Short vertical line to edge of stone, one on each side 6 in or 7 in long at 45° to the vertical. (4) Fifth course. Stylehole in mortar line. No circle; vertical line 5–6 in long ending in deep hole like stylehole. Three or four irregular radii in left quadrant ending in holes. (5) Sixth course. Small stylehole in stone; no circle. Four or five faint lines in left quadrant ending in holes, vertical lines indistinct. (6) Ninth course right side. Large stylehole in stone, no circle of horizontal line. Nine faint lines about 5 in long at regular distances, four on each side of the vertical. (7) Ninth course, left side. Stylehole in stone. No circle or horizontal line, vertical line ending in hole. Eight or nine very faint lines. (8) Tenth course, large stylehole. No circles or lines but segment of circumference composed of small holes on left lower side of stylehole.

LAVERSTOKE PARK. Two dials. (1) On large stone over closed doorway in north wall of nave. Stylehole in centre of stone still retaining fragment of iron style. Four cut radii, one vertical, with one on each side at an angle of 10° to 15° to it, and a distinctly cut 9 o'clock line about 5 in long, the whole enclosed in a deeply incised upright parallelogram. (2) on the east face of the south-east angle of nave, about 4 ft above ground. Stylehole in stone, small and filled in. An indefinite number of faint lines radiating from it in all directions, including many later scratches. On the left side a semicircle of small holes 1 in apart, 7 in or 8 in from stylehole. Stone much weathered. The position of both these dials point to rebuilding.

MONK SHERBORNE. One dial on the south face of the projecting angle of nave in the angle of the south chancel wall and annexe. Stylehole in stone. Full circle, 7 in diameter of equidistant holes. Horizontal line distinct. Lines dividing lower semicircle into 12 equal parts and all ending in holes. Vertical line extended upwards towards circumference, the whole dial inclining 20° to the right indicating removal of stone .

NORTH WALTHAM. Trace of dial left side of south chancel doorway, about 2 ft 6 in above ground. Shallow stylehole; no circle or horizontal lines. Five or six faint holes arranged in semicircle 5 in from stylehole with very faint connecting lines.

PRESTON CANDOVER. Dial on south doorway of mortuary chapel, formerly chancel of Parish Church. On the bottom course left side of door. Stylehole in stone, full circle 6 in diameter. Lower semicircle divided by lines into twelve equal parts. Two lines on right weathered to indistinctness.

SHERBORNE ST. JOHN. Five dials. (1) Over south doorway, now under Tudor porch. Stylehole in mortar line above keystone; horizontal line on left only, vertical line running to lower edge of keystone. Three lines on either side of vertical 10–12 in long, but 9 o'clock line is distinguished by being 18–20 in long. This dial is slightly inclined to the left. (2) On south wall of porch right side of door, about 3 ft up. Stylehole in stone, full circle 8 in diameter. Horizontal line with seven lines below it dividing semicircle into eight equal parts. These lines have been extended by scratching across the upper semicircle. This dial also is slightly inclined to the left. (3) On the south face of the southwest angle of nave, about 9 ft up. Stylehole in stone, with full circle 7–8 in diameter. Horizontal line with five lines below it, dividing lower semicircle into six equal parts. Vertical line is extended upwards to circumference and also beyond circle on the lower side, where the projection has a short cross line below circle. (4) On the south face of the south-east angle of nave about 4 ft up. Large and deep stylehole in stone. Horizontal line doubtful. Six lines in all, one vertical with two equally spaced on each side and a very distinct 9 o'clock line, all lines being short, broadly and deeply cut. (5) Trace of dial on east face of the south-east angle of chancel about 2 ft up. Stylehole and radii very shallow and hardly visible. The position and apparent inclination of this dial indicates removal of stone in rebuilding.

STEVENTON. Four dials. One on west doorway, three on south-west angle of nave. (1) Right side of door 4 ft up. Stylehole in mortar line. No circle. A number of lines 3–5 in long apparently dividing lower semicircle into 12 equal parts. Damaged by later scratching. (2) On the south face of south-west angle of nave about 5 ft 6 in up. Stylehole in stone, full circle about 8 in diameter. Definite horizontal line. Lower semicircle originally divided into eight equal parts. All rays end in holes on the circle. All this original work was well carved, but three later lines in the power and several in the upper part of the circle have been roughly scratched in. (3) About 18 in below (2). Stylehole in stone. Faint semicircle 8 in diameter. Shallow stylehole. Eight equidistant rays like wheel spokes each ending in a hole. Several intermediate scratched lines.

UP-NATELY. Dial on the window ledge of the south-east chancel window. Stylehole in stone on the line of junction between face of stone and window splay, which forms horizontal line. Two semicircles $\frac{1}{2}$ in apart, 8 in diameter. Lines divide semi-circle into 12 equal parts, but much weathered.

WINCHFIELD. Dial on the right side of south porch door 3 ft up. Stylehole in stone, probably full circle 8 in diameter but now very faint. Vertical line distinct, with traces of others, of which only two are clear. Inverted in rebuilding. Small copy dial below.

(iii) *ROYAL VISITS*

1226—*King Henry III* passed a night on his way to Reading (Friend of Walter de Merton).

1285—*King Edward I* stayed at Basing.

1499—*King Henry VII* visited Basingstoke in September.

1509—*Catherine of Aragon* slept at the house of Mr. Kingsmill, leaving the next day for Dogmersfield, where she met *King Henry VIII* to whom she was betrothed.

? *King Edward VI* stayed at Basing for four days.

1554—*Prince Philip of Spain* and *Queen Mary* spent five days at Basing after their wedding in Winchester Cathedral.

1560—*Queen Elizabeth I* was entertained at Basing House.

1592—*Queen Elizabeth I* visited the Chapel of the Holy Ghost.

1601—*Queen Elizabeth I* again visited Basing.

(iv) *STREET NAMES OF THE BOROUGH*

ALDWORTH CRESCENT—named after Richard Aldworth, Alderman of the City of London, who was a very wealthy citizen and among whose bequests was one to found a "Blue Coat School" in Basingstoke. The funds of the Aldworth bequest are now dispensed by Trustees who award grants for scholarships for higher education to local students.

ALEXANDRA ROAD—associated with royalty, name chosen by the developer when this and neighbouring roads were built.

BAYNARD'S CLOSE—George Baynard was one of the bailiffs appointed under the Charter of James I and was also the first Mayor under the Charter of Charles I.

BEACONSFIELD ROAD—doubtless commemorates the Victorian statesman but his association with Basingstoke, if any, is unknown.

BEDFORD PLACE—the Duke of Bedford lived in Bedford House which gave its name to this road which was formerly called Little Lane.

BOLTON CRESCENT—is so named from the Bolton family who lived at Hackwood House and owned the estate at Old Basing.

BOUNTY ROAD—named after May's Bounty, the appropriate name for the cricket ground which was the gift of Col. John May.

BOWER STREET—may get its name from an orchard, near the Old Bell Inn in 1661.

BROCAS ROAD—the Brocas family held the estate of Beaurepaire at Bramley for many generations. (See also mention of the family in chapter VI).

BROOK STREET—obvious and natural name for the road following alongside the Town Brook which still runs (mostly underground now) from west to east. The name has varied over the years once being Frog Lane at the western end and Water Lane towards Basing, sometimes all being called North Brook Street.

BUNNIAN PLACE—named from Bunny's Bars which used to be a gate; there may be a connection with Thomas Bunny who was a warden of the Holy Ghost Guild in 1604.

BURGESS ROAD—named after a one-time Mayor, John Burgess Soper.

CASTLE ROAD—traditionally there was a castle somewhere in the Fairfields area, earlier referred to as Castle Field.

CASTONS ALLEY—previously Bishop's Alley, named after Aaron Caston, ironmonger whose premises were on the site of the Town Hall.

CASTONS ROAD—see Castons Alley.

CHAPEL STREET—takes its name from being the approach for many generations to the Holy Ghost Chapel; previously known as "Hollie Goste Street" or the White Way, possibly because of the much used track being worn down to the chalk subsoil.

CHEQUERS ROAD—probably got its name from the Anchor Inn in London Street which was originally known as The Chequers and which owned land where Chequers Road now is.

CHESTERFIELD ROAD—named after the Chairman of the Housing Committee in 1927, whose scheme included the construction of this road.

CHURCH LANE—part of an old long path leading from St. Michael's Church to Tunworth Church.

CHURCH STREET—name presumably goes back earlier than St. Michael's Church and most likely refers to the track leading to Chapel Street and the Holy Ghost Chapel.

CORONATION ROAD—most likely commemorating the Coronation of Edward VII.

CRANBOURNE LANE—means Heron Brook; its earlier name was Combe Way.

CROMWELL ROAD—possibly commemorates Cromwell's occasional visits to the town, while at Basing.

DARLINGTON ROAD—no known local association.

DEEP LANE—joined the Upper and Lower Ways; was probably a deeply cut cart track as far back as the sixteenth century, before any buildings were erected in the vicinity.

DOSWELL WAY—name of the Mayor during four years of the Second World War.

EASTFIELD AVENUE—one of the large open fields that surrounded the town from the thirteenth century.

EASTROP LANE—named after the parish of Eastrop, a parish with a curiously remote detached portion between Up-Nately and Greywell called locally Strip Farm.

ESSEX ROAD—one of the roads built by Mr. Tyrrell of Old Basing, who had lived in Essex in a house called Solby's, and he named these roads after his old home area.

FAIRFIELDS ROAD—this land was given to the Corporation in 1786 as replacement for land at Kempshott, enclosed under the Enclosure Act, where the town's fairs had originally been held.

FENCOTT PLACE—built by James Fencott, a personal friend of John Burgess Soper.

FLAXFIELD ROAD—bears a very old name, "le Flexacre", first being mentioned about 1300.

FOULFLOOD LANE—also an ancient name, dating from Saxon times when the valley bottom was wet and marshy far above its present spring head.

FRANCES ROAD—name of the wife of the developer.

GEORGE STREET—see Alexandra Road.

GOAT LANE—seems to have taken its name from its Inn, The Goat. Its original name was Haine's Lane, named after an old Basingstoke family.

GREENWAY—restores to daily use the name that the road bore in 1407, and which had been lost for centuries "the Greenway leading from the highway to Wylknysshbury".

HACKWOOD ROAD—a directional name, formerly Hackwood Lane or Duke Street.

HARROW WAY—easily the earliest and oldest name, dating from pre-Saxon times. See also chapter I.

HILLARY ROAD—retains the name of the Mayor from 1909–10 who rendered excellent public service.

JACOBS ALLEY—so called from a harness maker called Jacobs who had his business on the east side of its London Street entrance. Formerly known as Common Alley, it may have been an easy pedestrian access to the Common.

JUBILEE ROAD—recalls the Jubilee of George III, which left its name on Jubilee Field. It was though, developed at the time of Queen Victoria's Jubilee in 1887.

KINGSCLERE ROAD—a directional name.

LANCASTER ROAD—recalls Sir James Lancaster, whose gratitude to his birthplace of Basingstoke is still shown today by the income the Corporation receives from his bequest made in the seventeenth century. (See Appendix 1.)

LEFROY AVENUE—records the name of well-known local men, associated with the Austens at Steventon. Mr. Christopher E. Lefroy lived at West Ham House and was the first president of the Mechanics' Institute. More recently, Mr. W. C. Lefroy of Goldings Park was the first Chairman of the Governors of the Girls' High School, and wrote their School Song.

LONDON STREET—together with WINCHESTER STREET, originally known as Bower Street, Bury Street, and the London Road, later to be split into two directional names.

LYFORD ROAD—another family sometime connected with Jane Austen and her family. Giles Lyford was three times Mayor in the late eighteenth century. John Lyford was a practising surgeon and man-midwife at the same time. Later Charles Lyford was Mayor in 1837, and the Mayoral Badge and Chair were his gifts to the Corporation.

MAY PLACE—named after John May of Odiham, who owned land in the area. Tradition decrees that he bought the land with golden guineas he found in the trunk of a tree which he felled.

MAY STREET—more modern name for the old cart track across Longcroft, a local field name. Col. John May, Mayor and benefactor of Basingstoke gave his name to the road. (See also Bounty Road.)

MERTON ROAD—the only visible link with the great Walter de Merton of the thirteenth century. (See also the Chapter on Walter de Merton.)

NEW ROAD—merely a description of a new road.

NEW STREET—a corruption of its original name of Stew Lane, running from Cow Cross Lane (later Cross Lane) to Allen's Lane (now Victoria Street).

NORDON CLOSE—shortened form of North Down, which was once the name of the district.

NORN HILL—as Nordon Close.

PARKSIDE ROAD—unimaginative name for road bordering Goldings Park.

PEMERTON ROAD—the name of a seventeenth century clothier, who left £100 for the relief of struggling fellow craftsmen. When the cloth trade died locally, his bequest was incorporated with those of Messrs. Payne and Stocker.

POTTERS LANE—suggests a pottery, as yet undiscovered.

QUEEN MARY AVENUE—relates to the return of Queen Mary's School to its original locality. See Chapter XI.

QUEEN'S ROAD—associations with Royalty; see Alexandra Road.

RALEIGH ROAD—see Essex Road.

READING ROAD—a directional name.

RICHMOND ROAD—no known local association.

ROCHFORD ROAD—see Essex Road.

ROUNDMEAD ROAD—originally Reighemede. The area still bears a rent charge left by Mr. J. Hall for the distribution of bread at the Parish Church.

RUSSELL ROAD—name of a distinguished local family, related to the Duke of Bedford.

SANDYS ROAD—the famous name of the family who lived for many generations at The Vyne, Sherborne St. John. See Chapter XI.

SARUM HILL—a directional name (Salisbury), originally Chitty's Hill, it used to be the dividing line between town and country.

SHERBORNE ROAD—a directional name.

SKIPPETTS LANE—preserves the name of the famous Skippers Inn on the Harrow Way. See Chapter XII.

SOLBY'S ROAD—see Essex Road.

SOPER GROVE—named after a one-time Mayor, John Burgess Soper.

SOUTHEND ROAD—see Essex Road.

SOUTHERN ROAD—replaces the name of the old Back Lane or Butt Lane, a farm road leading to paddocks and fields which lay between it and the London Road.

STATION HILL—obviously of recent date, having been set across open fields to the "new" station in 1839.

VICTORIA STREET—in honour of Queen Victoria.

VYNE ROAD—is the southern end of the footpath that runs to The Vyne at Sherborne St. John.

WALLIS ROAD—commemorates the name of the family justly famous for the service its members have rendered to the town in the promotion of its culture, education and industry.

WARTON ROAD—named after the Vicar of Basingstoke from 1723–45, one Thomas Warton, and his two even more famous sons, Joseph, Vicar of Winslade, Vicar of Tunworth, later Headmaster of Winchester College, and Thomas, Poet Laureate.

WINDOVER STREET—name of a farmer Thomas Windover in late eighteenth century.

WINCHESTER STREET—a directional name. (See also London Street.)

WORTING ROAD—directional, originally being called the Upper Way to Worting, the Lower Way being West Ham.

WOTE STREET—a puzzle in its modern spelling. From the sixteenth century at least, it was called Ote Street, a hundred years ago it was definitely Oat Street.

Index